GOD?

GOD?

DONNA M. YOUNG

God?
Copyright © 2020 by Donna M. Young. All rights reserved.

No part of this publication may be reproduced, stored in a retrieval system or transmitted in any way by any means, electronic, mechanical, photocopy, recording or otherwise without the prior permission of the author except as provided by USA copyright law.

Unless otherwise indicated, all Scripture quotations are from *The Holy Bible, English Standard Version*®, copyright © 2001 by Crossway Bibles, a publishing ministry of Good News Publishers. Used by permission. All rights reserved.

Published by Donna M. Young
  P O Box 76, Lawton, IA 51030
  dmywriting@wiatel.net

Author photo by Elizabeth Rose Kahl

Book Cover and Layout by Christina Hicks
christinahickscreative@gmail.com

Published in the United States of America
softcover #978-1-947143-18-0
e-book #978-1-947143-19-7
Non-Fiction / General
Non-Fiction / Christian General

http://www.donnamyoungwriting.com

Table of Contents

Introduction. 9

The Same God? 19

Why Do Bad Things Happen
to Good People?. 103

Why Does God Allow Suffering? 119

Why Must I Forgive? 141

Does God Still Perform Healings
and Other Miracles?. 147

How About Tongues? Are They Real?
Should We Speak in Tongues? 153

Is Satan Real and Are There Actual Places
Called Hell and Heaven? 165

Why Would a Loving God Condemn
People to Hell?. 171

Who Created God? 175

Is God an Uncaring Egomaniac? 185

How Can You Possibly Believe in a
6 Day Creation Scenario? What
About Evolution? 191

Do You Believe We Are Facing an
Impending Climate Catastrophe? What
is Our Duty, as Christians, to the Earth
God has Given Us for a Habitation?...... 209

Does God Get Mad When We are Angry
With Him, Or When We Doubt Him? ... 219

Should Christians be Involved
in Politics? 239

What Does God Think About
Abortion?............................ 253

How Does God Feel About
Homosexuality? 275

How Many Genders Did God Create? 297

What About Marriage. Does God
Care Who We Marry? 309

What is the Unpardonable Sin? 313

Is the Bible True and Reliable? 321

What is My Purpose? 369

Why am I Here?. 383

7 Prophesies Which Must be Fulfilled
Before the Coming of Christ 385

Introduction

We are indeed living in perilous times, just look around. Pandemics shutting down our world economy. Riots, looting and violence razing towns and cities across our country, abortion on demand killing our precious unborn, new euthanasia proponents springing up in positions of power and natural disasters wreaking havoc on the land.

Blatant hatred and division seem to be the theme of the day, often promoted by those who would destroy our society for their own political profit, or monetary gain. I'm sure the Father weeps. He yearns for us to trust Him and give ourselves wholly to Him. He created one race, 'humanity'. And just as He desires that we would each come to know Jesus as Savior, He also desires emphatically for us to love one another as He loves us, unconditionally, not dependent on the color of our skin, our political differences, our place of origin, or indeed, even our religion.

Political correctness has twisted our ability to see straight. People are literally scared to death to speak the truth for fear of being called "racist", "homophobic", "xenophobic" and the like. Honesty, in many cases, has taken a back seat to other's opinions of us. What a sad commentary on the state of our country and our world.

I have heard many people comment that they see the book of Revelation playing out before their eyes and I would tend to agree that it certainly looks as if the end is near. Though none of us knows the exact day or time when Jesus will return, we do know that multitudes of end time prophecies contained in the Word of God have already been fulfilled. Around fifty years ago we were told by bible experts that there were seven remaining biblical prophecies that must be accomplished before His coming. Some of which, in this modern age, have already come to pass and some which seem poised to be fulfilled. I have included these seven prophesies to which I refer later in the book for you to examine.

I am thrilled about the prospect of the Lord's return. Eternity with Jesus will be an indescribable blessing. How do I know this is unquestionably my own destiny? Because He told me in His Word that to achieve that end, I must believe He is the Son of God and that He died to save me from my sin. I understand that I must confess my sin, believe on Him and invite Him into my life to be my Savior and Lord. Indeed, I have, I do, and I have with great joy. What a wonderful gift.

I will grant that there are issues of concern, especially in these tumultuous days. Even more so for those who have yet to invite Jesus into their hearts. For this reason, I sincerely recommend to those who do not know Christ as Lord and Savior that you take this opportunity to welcome Him into your life with open arms. For there is nowhere He would rather be than in the hearts of His beloved children.

For those who are already Christians, this scenario of end times is not nearly as frightening a concept, nor should it be, as it is for those who do not know our Messiah in a personal way. From where does our confidence arise? Our confidence is in the Lord. He is still God; He is still on the throne and those of us who know His Word also know that we can safely depend on Him for our present situations and ultimately for our eternity.

In our ministry my husband, Pastor Marty, and I are faced with questions every day from non-believers, but we are also confronted by many inquiries that come from confused believers. In this book, "God?", I intend to address some of the most common questions we've encountered throughout the years. Using pertinent scriptures, we will get to the bottom of those biblically important issues and hopefully help those who are questioning, with answers that will bring them closer to a sense of peace in a perilous time.

If you are not Christian, you might think my answers trite. I sincerely hope not. I do this work with the most loving of intents and purposes. God doesn't want anyone lost and neither do I. You might think these answers not solid enough to alter your existing mindset, especially if your thought is based on worldly thinking. However, my evidence comes by way of a Christian perspective and a Christian world view. From there will I make my stand. A stand that I sincerely hope will win your heart for Jesus.

As a Christian, I believe the Bible to be the inerrant, infallible Word of God and the ultimate answer to every single question encountered by man. So, obviously, my proof will be found in His Word, the Bible. There are a great many answers in this invaluable resource if we will only seek them out.

My objective in penning "God?" is to enrich

and not to tear down. I seek merely to enlighten in a culture that seems hell bent on pulling people as far away from salvation in Christ as possible. And sadly, from recent PEW polls, it is working. According to a poll from 2019, as compared with their 2018 and 2015 polls, Christianity is in rapid decline. Fewer Americans identify as Christians and even fewer relate that they attend church on any kind of regular basis. Such a sad statement is a land which was founded in Christian, Judeo values.

I am certainly not out to disparage another's culture, religion, or thought process. Though, as a Christian, I would certainly love to see every person on earth come to realize the peace which can only come from knowing Jesus.

In the end each of us must discover that

which will give us an unquestionable peace. For my mind, that peace comes only from The Lord Jesus Christ, my God and my Savior.

My answers to the following questions are not based on, or derived from, my own opinions. Though I will admit that were I to be questioned on these upcoming subjects I would always agree with God's determinations. I would rather stand with the Lord and be judged by man, than stand with man and be judged by the Lord. Instead, each carefully researched answer is based on information gleaned from the Bible and other easily accessible resources. So, if you disagree with the sometimes controversial answers you see in these pages, I might suggest you take it up with the Lord.

I have decided to answer unapologetically

all the questions posed, since these answers are available to everyone, by reading God's Word, and should need no apology from me or anyone else.

As we delve into the Bible and the holy books of other world religions and denominations, comparing them with the Word of Jehovah God, looking for the answers to our burning questions and seeking the ultimate truth where it may be found, let us strive to know and then share that Truth with every creature.

"For God so loved the world, that He gave His only Son, that whoever believes in Him should not perish but have eternal life."

John 3:16

The Same God?

The scripture which opens this chapter is probably one of the most recognizable and beloved scriptures in all of Christendom and likely one of the most often encountered in the world at large. Yet, of all the questions we hear in daily ministry, one of the most common is: #Does any of it really matter? We're all praying to the same god anyway, aren't we?

In studying the major religions and Christian denominations of the world we have done our fair share of research on the subject and I would have to say that the short answer to that question is, no. No, we are not all praying to the same God 'as He defines Himself and our path to Him', in His own Holy Word. However, the long answer will require some pertinent information about many different religions and denominations. For that reason, I will be offering sub-chapters on each religion and denomination, to show the differences in what these religions and denominations believe about who our Christian God is, in comparison to the gods of other belief systems.

Additionally, I will show you what the gods, who represent each brand of spirituality, expect, offer and espouse. Most of all, we will search out God's ultimate and final Word, concerning salvation. This should, ultimately, make for a less confusing answer to this very important question.

In developing appropriate answers, I have done exhaustive research into the holy books and websites of other religions and denominations. I have also sought out devoted members of these various religions and denominations, some of whom spoke to me freely and some who were a bit more guarded. Then I realized it might be informative to also tap into the knowledge of some local religious leaders, from faiths other than Christianity.

Both the Muslim Imam and the Jewish Rabbi I spoke with vehemently declared that there is indeed only one god. Allah, or Jehovah, respectively. I was informed that we are certainly all praying to the same god. That is, if we (as Christians) will only denounce the very idea that our God has a son. Because, in both cases, their god has no son. The problem with this answer lays in the fact that the centrality of Christianity is based upon the fact that our Christian God does have a Son, Jesus, the very Name of God that has been revealed to us in Holy Scripture. Jesus Christ, the Savior of the world. To denounce that fact would make us, well, un-Christian.

So, why is it then that so many believe we are praying to the same god? I believe it is a notion promulgated by those in our midst (primarily globalists), who for many years have been nudging our nation toward the idea of a one world government, a one world religion and ultimately a godless, communist or socialist society. Those sources have been trying desperately to remove Jesus from the equation for a very long time. From our schools, the town square, our government buildings and our entertainment sources. Those same forces who push for a one world order, a one world government and a one world currency (a cashless society) would like to see us "praying" to one god, even if that god is a false one, because it would be much easier to eliminate the idea of God altogether, if we lump Him in with all the other false idols of the world.

This very thing has been accomplished in every communist and socialist society in the world. By first forcing the one true God out, ultimately channeling the masses into a government instituted 'religion' of sorts and then telling them what they must think and believe. Once their so-called religion is no longer one of a personal nature with the "One True God" it is much easier to extinguish what remains of their faith all together.

Yes, the very thing that distinguishes Christianity from every other religion is the claim that God does indeed have a Son. A perfect

Son who came to earth as a man, suffered and died on a cross for our sins, my sins and yours, rose from the grave on the third day to overcome that sin and who sits at the right hand of God the Father in heaven as our mediator with the Father.

Christianity is the only religion on earth that claims a Savior who paid a debt He didn't owe, so that we might have the gift of salvation, freely given, for any who would just believe on Him. The only religion where the seeker does not sacrifice anything at all, not a single thing, except his arrogant, self-centered belief that he can somehow be good enough to attain eternity with the Father entirely on his own. I am continually amazed at this faith we follow, where love plus nothing else saves.

You see, if those who seek our submission

and ultimately our destruction, can dissuade us from the righteous path of following Christ, by making Him unimportant and unnecessary, then a one world religion and ultimately that one world order is more easily within their grasp.

If we are Christian, Jesus Christ is the very core of our Christian belief. Without the Son of God there is no Christianity. Without Him being God's greatest gift to us there is no salvation. Yet, in Islam for instance, I was able to find at least twenty-one separate surahs (verses) in the Quran that say God has no son, along with the warning that to assert that He does have a son is blasphemy and that we should desist from this claim for our own good. So, here we go. Let's discover the core beliefs of these major religions and denominations, so that we might determine the facts for ourselves.

A reminder: These answers are not derived from my own personal opinions, but from the Holy Bible, the Holy Books of the religions and denominations in question and in many cases, the websites linked to those religions and denominations.

Islam

Muslims believe that Jesus lived and was indeed the son of Mary. A fact that would be difficult to escape due to the overwhelming proof of a historical Jesus. However, Mohammad claims He was no more than a messenger, a mere prophet.

As I stated previously, I found at least twenty-one surahs in the Quran stating that God does not have a Son. If you have never read the Quran or the Hadiths, which are the Muslim holy writings, it is an eye opening and sometimes quite shocking experience to do so. One example I found was Surah 4:171 which goes like this: "O followers of the Book! Do not exceed the limits in your religion, and do not speak (lies) against Allah, but (speak) the truth; the Christ Jesus son of Mary is only an apostle of Allah and His word which He communicated to Mary and a spirit from Him; believe therefore in Allah and His apostles, and say not, Three. Desist, it is better for you; Allah is only one God: far be it from His glory that He should have a son; whatever is in the heavens and whatever is in the earth is His; and Allah is sufficient for a Protector."

There are other Surahs proclaiming the same.

Some of note are: 9:30, which reads, "And the Jews say, "Ezra is God's son," while the Christians say, "The Christ is God's son." Such are the sayings which they utter with their mouths, following in spirit assertions made in earlier times by people who denied the truth! They deserve the imprecation: "May God destroy them!" How perverted are their minds!"

Read also: 17:111, 19:35, 19:92, 25:2, 39:4 and many others.

This notion of dismissing Jesus, of denying His deity, plays right into the hands of Satan. Our greatest enemy will have us deny Jesus before men so that Jesus would deny us before the Father. Please don't fall into that trap.

Islam began six hundred years after the crucifixion of Christ. In recording the Quran

Mohammad and his scribes used many names from the Bible in these writings including those of Jesus and Mary. After all, an untruth is much easier to swallow when it is couched in bits of truth. Mohammad's assertion was that there are many holy writings. However, he believed the Quran was the more divine of the holy writings, as it was the conclusion of all divine revelations, especially for the family of Abrahamic faith: of the Torah revealed to Moses and the Bible (as he claims) later 'revealed' to Jesus. He did not hold with the notion that Jesus is The Word incarnate and that the words of the Bible flow directly from Him, in all their wonder and magnificence. That the entire Bible is God breathed.

The Quran asserts that there is not and never will be a "Son of God" to save us. How can one conclude from this evidence that we are praying to the same god? I declare we are not.

Judaism

The Tanakh, the Jewish holy book, which is the equivalent of the Bible's Old Testament, does indeed reveal Jehovah God, the Creator of the universe. Yes, the same Old Testament God that we, as Christians, call 'The Father'. And yes, He is Father God. However, Judaism would have us stop at the Old Testament and continue to wait. Because, for the Jews the prophesied Messiah has not yet come.

Though Christians and Jews both worship Jehovah God, their Jehovah does not have a son. Jesus, the Savior revealed in the New Testament, the Son of God is very real to those who hold

Christianity dear.

The Bible is replete with scripture referring to Jesus as the Son of God. Even Jesus Himself tells us He is indeed the Son of God. In a cursory examination of The Word I was able to find a minimum of fifty-eight scripture examples making this point. I have included a few:

1 John 5:20 "And we know that the Son of God has come and has given us understanding, so that we may know Him who is true; and we are in Him who is true, in His Son Jesus Christ. He is the true God and eternal life."

Luke 1:35 "And the angel answered her, "The Holy Spirit will come upon you, and the power of the Most High will overshadow you; therefore, the child to be born will be called holy – the Son of God."

John 5:18 "This was why the Jews were seeking all the more to kill Him, because not only was He breaking the Sabbath, but He was even calling God His own Father, making Himself equal with God."

John 1:14 "And the Word became flesh and dwelt among us, and we have seen His glory, glory as of the only Son from the Father, full of grace and truth."

John 14:10 "Do you not believe that I am in the Father and the Father is in me? The words that I say to you I do not speak on my own authority, but the Father who dwells in me does His work."

John 6:40 "For this is the will of my Father, that everyone who looks on the Son and believes in Him should have eternal life, and I will raise him up on the last day.

Mark 5:7 "And crying out with a loud voice, he (the demon) said, "What have You to do with me, Jesus, Son of the Most High God? I adjure You by God, do not torment me."

1 John 4:10 "In this is love, not that we have loved God but that He loved us and sent His Son to be the propitiation for our sins."

John 10:30 "I and the Father are one."

Here are a few other verses you might want to take the time to look up. Isaiah 9:6, Hebrews 5:5, Philippians 2:5-8, John 17:5, John 5:19, Hebrews 1:2, 1 Corinthians 15:28, and Romans 1:4. For Christians there are many more pieces of scripture that back up the undeniable fact that Jesus Christ is the Son of God. Please take the time to read and study the scriptures. When we are armed with the truth it is impossible for the enemy to pull the wool over our eyes. Equip yourself with godly knowledge and you will not be dissuaded by Satan's wily tricks.

If Christianity embodies the loving sacrifice of Jesus, the Son of God who came to save. And the Tanakh denies Jesus' very existence as that beloved Son of God, we must logically conclude that at the very least Judaism is stalled at the introduction of the New Testament. Perhaps we as Christians need to do a better job of evangelism concerning our Jewish friends.

Now, obviously, Messianic Jews who have come to saving grace in Christ, do believe that God has a Son. In that case Jesus is the answer and for those individuals who believe, we are certainly praying to the same God, Jehovah, praise His Holy Name.

Examining the fundamental beliefs of some additional world religions and denominations, to discover what drives them, let us see what is compatible and what is not.

Buddhism

About 2500 years ago a prince, Siddhartha Gautama, began to question his life of luxury and looked instead for a different path. In his searching he spent much time in meditation. One day, we are told, while sitting under a Poplar-Figtree in Bodh Gaya, India a realization came to him.

From there he developed his "Three Universal Truths", his "Four Noble Truths" and "The Eightfold Path". Principles he espoused to his followers for forty-five years. He spent a great deal of time in meditation and was said to have achieved Nirvana, or 'enlightenment'. Due to this he was given the title of "Buddha" or enlightened one.

The prince told his followers not to consider him a god, but to be responsible for their own lives and to follow the 'middle path' to enlightenment, to achieve Nirvana. Buddha did not consider himself god, and neither should we. However, as Christians, we also do not consider ourselves capable of attaining enlightenment on our own. As human beings we are inherently incapable of being good enough, when held up to the perfect example of God's law and due to that we ultimately need a Savior.

Therefore, since Christians know that our

God has a Son, who died for us to set us free from our sin and selfishness, we must certainly not be praying to the same god.

Hinduism

At approximately four-thousand years it is the oldest religion known to mankind. It began in India and today boasts around one billion adherents worldwide. Hinduism is the ancient belief of a people known as the Aryans, or "Noble people". Their philosophy, religion and customs are recorded in their sacred texts known as the Vedas.

Based on a foundational belief that a human being's nature is not confined to the body or the mind and that beyond both is the spark of God residing within the soul from the moment of creation.

The Bible tells a different story, which is that all humans are born into original sin. Due to that original sin, we are born spiritually dead within. The indwelling of the Holy Spirit comes only after confessing Jesus as Savior of our lives and inviting Him to live within our hearts.

Hinduism's claim is that this spark, or spirit, exists not only in humans, but in everything we see. In other words, all of creation is imbued with the same spark or spirit as the creator, as one huge mass of spiritual being. Christianity has a different view. In Romans 1:21-25 we read, "For although they knew God, they did not honor him as God or give thanks to him, but they became futile in their thinking, and their foolish hearts were darkened. [22] Claiming to be wise, they became fools, [23] and exchanged the glory of the immortal God for images resembling mortal man and birds and animals and creeping things. [24] Therefore God gave them up in the lusts of their hearts to impurity, to the dishonoring of their bodies among themselves, [25] because they exchanged the truth about God for a lie and worshiped and served the creature rather than the Creator, who is blessed forever! Amen.

Brahman, god's name in Hinduism, also addressed as Atman, Shiva, Vishnu, Kali, Durga, or a multitude of other 'divine' names (with a multitude of images resembling various persons or creatures). All of whom may be prayed to for help and protection, is the same as the divine essence, or 'spark' that resides in every created thing. Thereby giving Hindis the freedom to pray to whatever manifestation of this divine spark that they wish in order to ask for assistance. In some sects there are literally tens of thousands of variations of the divine.

Multiple sects of Hinduism, each a bit different, all follow the fundamental teachings of the religion as taught in the concluding portion of the Vedas, the Vedanta, or the Upanishads. In their religious training everyone is taught to undergo steps necessary to purify and refine the mind and senses. This training is accomplished through various forms of yoga.

In true Christianity we pray to God, through Jesus Christ, only. We are aware that we are only purified through the blood of Jesus and the work He alone accomplished on the cross.

The concept of reincarnation is also a difference worthy of note. Hinduism teaches that we are each responsible for the results of our actions and that we can create a better tomorrow by resolving to do better today. Through this thinking, when one dies, they can be reborn into a lower or higher life contingent upon the actions of their previous life.

Christians believe that through the sacrifice, once for all, of Jesus on the cross; and if we confess Him as Savior and Lord; we will dwell with Him forever when we leave this earthly life.

Hindus follow a code of behavior determined by their place in society and the duties associated with it. Brahmins are priests and teachers; Kshatriyas are rulers and soldiers. Vaishyas are merchants and Shudras are workers. Each occupies a rung on the ladder of society from high born to low (the caste system) with certain expectations, and those of a low status, in this present life, cannot ever hope to obtain a higher position in that caste system.

Christianity teaches us that God loves us all and died for all of mankind. As Christians we also believe that the gift of salvation is available to every person, no matter their status, former mistakes, or previous positions. None of us can do anything to earn it and it can't be bought. We believe there is one race, which includes all of humanity, created equal in His eyes. We are taught to love one another as He loves us.

Hindus and Christians are not praying to the same god.

Druidism

Of mostly unknown origin and age this ancient way of life is free from most of the dogma and fixed beliefs of most religions. Druids do not have a holy text, such as a Bible, Quran, or Vedas and their beliefs vary to some degree.

Woven into much of Druid thought is the idea that we are all connected in a universe that is essentially benign, that we are not isolated beings. Instead, part of a great web of fabric which includes every living creature and all of nature and creation, thereby making all things in nature equal in value, including human beings. Hence, Druids reverence all of nature as holy and the life of a human being of no more worth than an insect or a tree.

Druids of different sects believe in either a god

of nature, a nature goddess, or a pairing of the two.

As Christians we are aware that God, in Genesis 1:26-31, gave dominion of the earth and all that is in it to mankind. The trees, plants, fish birds and creatures of the fields are not made equal to man. Now, that said, we are to be good stewards of that which God has given us to tend and I will admit that some fall horribly short in that regard. However, God has not told us to worship, or even reverence these created things. We are to worship Him and Him alone.

Druids and Christians do not pray to the same god.

Wicca

I won't delve too deeply into this one. Made up of covens, which ideally number ten to fifteen members, those who call themselves followers of Wicca practice witchcraft and worship nature. They believe in the "Goddess" and revere her as they revere nature. As coven members master the practice of magic and become familiar with the rituals, they pass through two degrees of initiation. There is a third-degree for those who wish to enter the priesthood.

Christians and those who practice Wicca do not pray to the same god.

Daoism

Alternately spelled, Taoism, this is an indigenous semi-religious, philosophical tradition followed by Chinese for more than two thousand years. Daoism, in the broadest sense embraces the joyful and carefree. It is also characterized by a positive, active attitude toward the occult and the metaphysical (theories on the nature of reality).

The Daoist religion, which revolves around the ritual worship of the Dao, drives much of Chinese thought and culture. In Chinese religion, the Daoist tradition, which often serves as a link to the Confucian and folk traditions, has generally been more popular and spontaneous than the official Confucian state cult, which is not really a religion as such.

Behind all forms of Daoism stands the figure of 'Laozi', regarded as the author of the classic text known as the Laozi, or the Daodejing (Classic of the Way of Power). He is also mentioned in the Zhuangzi, named for its author. In this work Laozi is described as one of Zhuangzi's teachers.

In these writings Laozi appears as a senior contemporary of Confucius. A renowned Daoist master, curator of the archives at the court of the Zhou dynasty and, finally, most important, a mere mortal.

Christians and Taoists do not pray to the same god.

Confucianism

Confucianism was not founded by Confucius, but in antiquity before him. The Lunyu (Analects) the most-revered sacred scriptures in the Confucian tradition, was most likely compiled by following generations of his disciples.

Confucius considered himself a teacher of humanity. His vision was to develop a moral community by restoring a trust in government and transforming society by cultivating a sense of humanity in politics. Confucianism, though always more a way of life than anything resembling a religion, has taken on a more modern transformation. Scholars in mainland China have also explored the possibility of a fruitful interaction between Confucian humanism and democratic liberalism in a socialist context.

Confucianism does not pray to any god.

Baha'i Faith

I almost didn't mention this one, since this religion has only five to eight million adherents worldwide. Then a friend of mine reminded me that her daughter had been caught up in this belief system for several years before coming to know Christ.

GOD?

Established in 1863, the Baha'i Faith has three central figures: the Bab (1819-1850) considered a herald who declared that God would soon send a "prophet" in the same way of Jesus or Muhammad. He was executed by Iranian authorities in 1850. Baha'u'llah (1817-1892), who claimed to be that prophet in 1863 and spent most of his life in prison and exiled. His son, Abdu'l-Baha' (1844-1921), who was released from confinement in 1908 and made teaching trips to Europe and America. Following Abdu'l-Baha's death in 1921, leadership of the religion fell to his grandson Shoghi-Effendi (1897-1957).

Baha'i teachings are like other monotheistic faiths. God is single and all-powerful. He does not have a son. Baha'u'llah taught that religion is orderly and progressively revealed by "manifestations" of God, who are the "founders" of major world religions throughout history; Buddha, Jesus and Mohammad being the most recent before Bab and Baha'u'llah. Jesus being a simple messenger like all the rest, with no more significance than any other messenger. The Baha'i Faith has a goal of unifying all people through a unified world order that ensures the prosperity of all nations, races, creeds and classes.

Obviously, without Jesus as God and central to all things, we are not praying to the same God.

Satanism

This one is a no brainer and should need no other explanation. Obviously, Christians and Satanists pray to a different god.

I would also like to touch on a couple of denominations that refer to themselves as Christian. Again, not to disparage, but simply to clarify for anyone who might be concerned about the question, "Are we praying to the same God?". To each his own.

A subtle difference is still a difference. So, if the main thrust of Christianity is a knowledge that Jesus is the Son of God and that though He is the Son of God, He is also the embodiment of God who has come in the flesh to save humanity from their sin, then denominations which deviate from this simple but necessary truth are standing in contrast.

We, as Christians, believe also in a Triune God, Father, Son and Holy Spirit, three in one.

The way we become followers of Christ, or

Christians if you will, is that we confess Jesus as the Son of God, admit that we are sinners, claim that He died for ME and that I desire for Him to come and live in my heart to be the Lord of my life. We must then logically conclude that if any other religion or denomination espouses any other deity, or any other way, as 'The Way' to the Father, our thoughts are not the same and we are not praying to the same god.

As I said previously, I am not out to disparage any other religion, but simply to share facts. Every fact I share is easily accessible by taking the time to read the holy writings of each individual religion, and in some cases as easy as accessing their website. Every person, when presented with these facts must make decisions that will give them the greatest amount of inner peace on the subject.

Having said this, there are even denominations within what we refer to as the Christian faith realm that claim things contrary to the elemental Biblical facts listed above. Let's examine these to see what we find.

Mormonism

Though Mormons consider themselves Christians they claim that their founding in 1830 was the beginning of a restored church that overcame the, so called, apostasy following apostolic times. However, if this were true, one would expect to find first century historical evidence for Mormon doctrines, such as the plurality of gods and God the Father having once been a man. All such evidence is completely lacking.

Yes, Mormons believe that God the Father was once a man who then progressed to godhood, which would mean that he is a now-exalted, immortal man with a flesh and bone body. The Bible does not back up this claim. Scripture tells us that God is not and has never been a man. See Scriptures: Numbers 23:19 "God is not man, that He should lie, or a son of man, that He should change His mind. Has He said, and will He not do it? Or has He spoken, and will He not fulfill it?"; Hosea 11:9 "I will not execute My burning anger; I will not again destroy Ephraim; for I am God and not a man, the Holy one in your midst, and I will not come in wrath."; He is a spirit (John 4:24) and a spirit does not have flesh and bones (Luke 24:39).

Additionally, God is eternal: Psalms 90:2; 102:27; Isaiah 57:15; 1 Timothy 1:7. He is also immutable, unchangeable in His being and perfection: Psalms 102:25-27; Malachi 3:6. He did not 'progress' toward godhood, but has, in fact, always been God.

Mormons are polytheists. They believe the Trinity consists not of three persons within one God, but rather three distinct gods. According to Mormonism, there are potentially thousands of gods besides these. However, as Christians, we know that trusting in or worshipping more than one God is explicitly condemned throughout the Bible: Exodus 20 "You shall have no other gods before me." There is only one true God: Deuteronomy 4:35, 39, 6:4; Isaiah 43:10, 44:6, 8, 45:18; 46:9; Corinthians 8:4; James 2:9; who exists eternally in three persons – the Father, the Son and the Holy Spirit: Matthew 28:19; 2 Corinthians 13:14.

Mormonism also teaches that humans can go through a process of exaltation to godhood, but the Bible teaches that the yearning to be godlike led to the fall of mankind, as we can read in Genesis 3:4-5 "But the serpent said to the woman," You will not surely die. For God knows that when you eat of it your eyes will be opened and you will be like God, knowing good and evil."

God does not look kindly on humans who pretend to attain to deity: Acts 12:21-23. He desires us to humbly recognize that we are His: Genesis 2:7, 5:2; Psalms 95:6-7. Our state, as the redeemed, in eternity will be one of glorious immortality. However, we will forever remain His creation, adopted as His children: Romans 8:14-30; 1 Corinthians 15:42-57; Revelation 21: 3 through 7. From these scriptures we can see that believers will never become gods.

Mormonism teaches that Jesus was the firstborn spirit-child of the heavenly Father and a heavenly Mother. They claim that He then progressed to deity in the spirit world. He was later physically conceived in Mary's womb, as the literal "only begotten" Son of God the Father in the flesh (though many present-day Mormons that I've spoken with, remain somewhat puzzled as to how this occurred).

Biblically, the description of Jesus as the "only begotten" refers to His being the Father's Unique, one-of-a-kind Son. He has the same divine nature as the Father: John 1:14; John:18, 3:16, 18; and John 5:18, 10:30. Additionally, He is eternal deity: John 1:1, 8:58; and is immutable: Hebrews 1:10-12, 13:8, which means that He did not progress to deity, but has indeed always been God. Moreover, Mary's conception of Jesus in His humanity was accomplished through a miracle of the Holy Spirit, as declared in Matthew 1:20.

Mormons believe that most individuals will wind up in one of three kingdoms of glory, depending on each person's degree of faithfulness. They further believe that belief in Christ, or even God for that matter, is not necessary to obtain immortality in one of these three kingdoms and therefore only the most spiritually perverse go to hell.

The Bible teaches only two possibilities for

our eternal future: the saved will have eternal life with God in the new heavens and new earth: Philippians 3:20; Revelation 21:1-4, 22:1-5; while the unsaved will find themselves spending an eternity in hell: Matthew 25:41; Revelation 20:13-15.

Mormons believe that Adam's transgression was a noble act that made it possible for humans to become mortal, which was a necessary step on the path of exaltation to godhood. Moreover, they think Christ's atonement secures immortality for effectively all people, whether they repent and believe (the one Biblically necessary component in the Bible) or not.

However, if we read Genesis 3:16-19 and Romans 5:12-14, we see that there was nothing noble about Adam's sin, which was not a stepping-stone to godhood but instead brought nothing but misery and death to mankind. Jesus alone atoned for the sins of all, but this gift is freely given 'only' to those who would trust Him for salvation: Isaiah 53:6; John 1:29; 2 Corinthians 5:21; 1 Peter 2:24, 3:18; 1 John 2:2, 4:10. In their tradition Mormons also believe God gives to virtually everyone a general salvation to immortal life in one of the three heavenly kingdoms. Belief in Christ is necessary only to obtain passage to the highest, celestial kingdom – for which not only faith, but participation in Mormon temple rituals and obedience to its "laws of the gospel" are also prerequisites.

For Christians, however, salvation by grace must be received only through faith in Christ: John 3:15-16, 11:25, 12:46; Acts 16:31; Romans

3:22-24; Ephesians 2:8-9. All true believers are promised eternal life in the presence of Almighty God: Matthew 5: 3 through 8; John 14: 1-3; and Revelation 21: 3-7.

Catholicism

The Roman Catholic church, with over a billion members worldwide, is the largest 'Christian' ecclesiastical body in the world.

Roman Catholic Bibles contain all the books one would find in a Protestant edition, though Catholicism also recognizes the collection of books called the Apocrypha to be within the canon of Holy Scripture. Protestants, on the other hand, read these books only as an example of life, or instruction of manners.

Roman Catholics, the Eastern Orthodox

and Protestants share quite a few core Christian beliefs, especially regarding the Trinity and the Incarnation. That said, faithful Roman Catholics also hold to several key distinctives.

One belief is that the Roman Catholic Church is the one true church. This comes from the view that their Pope occupies the episcopal seat of Peter and is the only vicar of Christ on earth. By their thinking, one must be Roman Catholic to attain heaven.

However, the Bible tells a different story. According to scripture one must confess that Jesus is the Son of God and that He died and rose again to pay for "MY" sins. Nowhere that I have been able to find in scripture is there a caveat that claims we must be of one denomination or another. We are simply required to believe: Acts

16:31 "They replied, "Believe in the Lord Jesus, and you will be saved – you and your household"; Romans 10:9-10 "If you declare with your mouth, "Jesus is Lord" and believe in your heart that God raised Him from the dead, you will be saved. For it is with your heart that you believe and are justified, and it is with your mouth that you profess your faith and are saved."; Romans 10:13 for "Everyone who calls on the Name of the Lord will be saved."; John 3:16 "For God so loved the world that He gave His one and only Son, that whoever believes in Him shall not perish but have eternal life."

Roman Catholics believe in purgatory, a state in the afterlife in which a Christian's sins are purged away, typically through suffering. If this were indeed true, why would Jesus necessarily have needed to die. This includes punishment for sins committed in one's earthly life. Understand their belief is that purgatory is sanctification extended even after death, until one is truly transformed and glorified in perfect holiness. They claim that all those in purgatory will reach heaven eventually. They do not remain there permanently and are never sent to the lake of fire.

On the other hand, the Bible tells us there are two destinations after death, heaven and hell. The first is reached by faith alone, through grace alone. BELIEVE. The second is the terrible cost of denying Jesus as the Son of God, Lord and Savior.

Another difference is the idea of a "treasury of merit." In a manner of speaking this is a sort of "bank" of grace. This is a place where the merits of Jesus and His Holy saints are stored, which can then be accessed for the benefit of other Christians. These merits never run out due to Christ's own infinite merit. Roman Catholics pray to Christ or any variety of saints, beseeching them for these benefits. One of the major controversies during the Protestant Reformation concerned the Pope's claim to have special access to this treasury of merit. The popes claimed that one could obtain 'indulgences from the Church, which would reduce the temporal punishment due for sins committed on earth. This meant shortening one's time in Purgatory. One could obtain indulgences for yourself, or a loved one. The popes allowed the sale and purchase of indulgences, typically to raise money for their elaborate buildings and other projects. This practice enraged theologians and pastors, including Martin Luther. Indulgences are still issued today, even though they are not commercialized as they were in the late medieval era thanks to reforms made in the Counter-Reformation.

Once again, I will say that the Bible is firm on the fact that there is only one way to the Father and that is through the Son, Jesus Christ: John 14:6 "Jesus said, "I am the Way, the Truth and the Life. No one comes to the Father except through Me."

With some exceptions, Roman Catholic clergy must remain celibate. This has been a mandatory policy since the Fourth Lateran Council (1215), though Peter (Catholicism's first Pope), was married Matthew 8:14-15. That same council mandated private oral confession for sin to a priest at least once a year and participation in Holy Communion to be sanctified. Neither of which is a condition expressed by Jesus in order to attain Grace.

Additionally, while all true Christians believe Jesus had an immaculate conception-that He was born free from the original sin inherited from Adam-Roman Catholics insist that Mary had a similar immaculate conception as a point of orthodoxy. Moreover, they believe her body was assumed-taken up-into heaven at the end of her earthly life, as her corpse has not been found. However, the Bible is adamant about not worshipping anything or anyone besides God the Father, through Jesus the Son: Exodus 20:4-5 "You shall not make for yourself an image in the form of anything in heaven above or on the earth beneath or in the waters below. You shall not bow down to them or worship them; for I, the Lord your God, am a jealous God, punishing the children for the sin of the parents to the third and fourth generation of those who hate me.

Regarding the Trinity, the Incarnation, and Christian morals, Roman Catholicism gets a lot of big things right. However, regarding doctrines of grace, salvation and authority, it gets a lot of big things wrong and can give us an understanding of why early Protestant documents included "anti-Christ" language about the Pope. Regardless, it behooves any Christian to know Roman Catholic beliefs, if only due to the church's size and influence.

I will leave it to you, as to whether we are praying to the same god.

Scientology

Scientology didn't start off as a religion. L. Ron Hubbard's Dianetics was more about counseling to remove unconscious scars that develop into negative memories. However, when Hubbard began to discuss "thetans", which are supposedly human immortal souls, Dianetics transitioned into Scientology.

There is much about Scientology that the noninitiate is not allowed to know. Secrets that only the higher tiers of Scientologists are privy to, but here are the facts that we do know.

According to Scientology's website there are three fundamental truths.

*Man is an immortal spiritual being.

*His experience extends well beyond a single lifetime.

*His capabilities are unlimited, even if not presently realized.

They believe that:

1. Human survival is the basic principle of existence. Things that lead to survival are good and pleasurable, while those things which are counter to our survival are negative.

2. Each person has an analytical mind in charge of making daily decisions and judgments necessary for survival. However, in times of stress or trauma, the reactive mind (subconscious) takes over. This action leaves scars on the reactive mind which are referred to as "engrams".

3. To rid an individual of "engrams", one must go through a process called "auditing".

Supposedly this process allows the analytical mind to regain control through a series of questions from a therapist and the use of an electropsychometer, or E-meter, (a device introduced by Hubbard which measures the strength of an electrical current running through an individual's body as that person answers the auditor's questions). It is claimed that the E-meter readings indicate changes in one's emotional state which allows the identification of engrams.

4. In Scientology, humans are immortal souls called "thetans" who are trapped in multiple bodies over various lifetimes. According to Hubard, thetans originated billions of years ago with the

"original Cause". Thetans, through their Interaction, created the physical universe of matter, energy, space and time. Over time, thetans fell into the physical universe and got trapped. They were slowly stripped of their creative abilities and the memory of who they were and ended up on earth.

5. Purging the mind of engrams, from all the lifetimes and events which robbed them of their creative abilities, causes a thetan to become "clear". Thetans who become clear reach a higher level of ethical and moral standards, are more creative with greater control of the environment and are less susceptible to disease. This is the goal of Scientology.

6. Clear thetans ascend to higher levels

in the church, becoming "Operating Thetans" or "OTs." they are also able to expand themselves by identifying with larger realities called "dynamics". A high-operating thetan can increase survival for all of Scientology's dynamics, which are: Infinity, Spiritual, Physical Universe, Life Forms, Mankind, Group Survival, Family and Self.

7. To a Scientologist all drugs are poisonous and inhibit spiritual freedom. To dislodge the toxins of drugs and chemical residues trapped in the body, one can participate in a "Purification Rundown", which includes sweating in a sauna, mega-vitamin regimens with minerals, good nutrition and extra oils, along with adequate rest.

8. The Creed of the Church of Scientology states, "And we of the Church believe That Man is basically good. That he is seeking to survive. That his survival depends upon himself and upon his fellows and his attainment of brotherhood with the Universe." Hubbard did not believe in the Christian God, but instead left everyone to come to their own conclusion about their god and his nature. Instead, focusing on helping members realize their own "inherent spiritual essence and abilities."

Scientology is not compatible with Christianity for a myriad of reasons. Here are the top five:

1. Christians put forth that humans exist for God, to glorify Him. Not, as Scientologists

claim, to merely survive.

2. Christians believe we die once. We do not believe that we live multiple lifetimes in multiple bodies. Hebrews 9:27 says, "People are destined to die once, and then face judgement."

3. Scientology asserts that, "Man is basically good". However, the Bible says, over and over, this is not so. Jerimiah 17:9 says, "The heart is deceitful above all things and beyond cure. Who can understand it?" Therefore, we need Jesus.

4. Scientology claims that a man's survival depends on himself and his attainment of brotherhood with the Universe." The Bible makes it abundantly clear that a person is incapable of saving him/herself.

In John 8:24, Jesus says, "I told you that you would die in your sins; if you do not believe that I am He (that is, the Son of God), you will indeed die in your sins."

Only by faith in Christ can we be saved. Acts 4:12 states, "Salvation is found in no one else, for there is no other name under heaven given to mankind by which we must be saved."

5. Though Scientology doesn't put emphasis on what a person believes about God, Christianity elevates God and seeks Him above all else.

I think it is clear we are not praying to the same god.

Unitarian Universalists

Unitarian Universalism describes itself as one of the most liberal religions. The UUA encourages its members to search for their own truth at their own pace. Embracing members of differing faiths, such as atheists, Buddhists, Christians and others, they borrow from many religions and do not have a creed or doctrinal requirements.

Belief in the Bible is not required, and we were told, when we asked, that, "The Bible is a collection of profound insights from the men who wrote it, but also reflects biases and cultural ideas from the times in which it was written and edited."

Universalists do not discriminate based on color, gender, sexual orientation or national origin. Some believe in God and others do not, as this is not a requirement. To them heaven and hell are states of mind, created by individuals and expressed by their actions. By their admission, Jesus was merely an outstanding human being, but divine only in that all humans possess a "divine spark". The UUA denies the Christian teaching that God required a sacrifice for atonement of sin. Though they recognize that human beings are capable of destructive behavior and that people should be responsible for their own actions, they reject the belief that Christ died to redeem humanity from sin.

Some UUA members pray, others meditate. And though they hold celebrations for coming of age, joining in marriage, dedicating children and commemorating the dead, their only true sacrament, I am told, is living life with justice and compassion. Sermons in a UUA service might contain information about their beliefs but are just as likely to be about controversial societal issues or politics.

Here I would say if an option is given that you don't have to believe in a god at all, we are not praying to the same god.

Christian Science

Mary Baker Eddy (the founder of Christian Science who passed away in 1910), when asked if Christian Scientists had a religious creed, answered, "They have not, if by that term is meant doctrinal beliefs" (Science and Health with Key to the Scriptures. Pp. 496-497). However, she did provide a few key points that briefly summarize the beliefs of Christian Science.

*Christian Scientists consider themselves to be adherents of Truth. They claim to take the inspired Word of the Bible as their sufficient guide to eternal life and accept its authority, though not its inerrancy. In other words, they deem the Bible to be written from the mind of man, rather than God inspired and God breathed. The Bible tells us in 2 Timothy 3:16-17 that all scripture is God breathed.

*Christian Scientists acknowledge one supreme and infinite God. They also accept the divinity of His Son, Jesus, but only in the way that His life would exemplify a divine sonship that makes all men and women His children equally. Additionally, they do not acknowledge the deity of Jesus, so He is the Son of God as we are all sons and daughters of God, but He is not God and King. They also recognize the Holy Ghost as the divine comforter, and man, in God's image and likeness. In John 10:22-30 Jesus tells us that He and the Father are one.

*Christian Scientists acknowledge God's forgiveness of sin in the destruction of sin and a spiritual understanding that casts out evil as unreal (their belief is that sin, along with all evil, is a state of mind). They also believe that the "imagined sin" that we might commit will be punished as long as the "belief of sin" is present, and we continue to dwell on it. So, sin is more a state of mind than a reality. In Romans 3:23, and Romans 5:12 we are told that ALL have sinned and fall short of the glory of God. That sin came into the world through one man (Adam) and that through sin death spread to everyone. Through these verses and others, it doesn't seem that God believes sin to be simply a state of mind which is not anchored in reality.

*They claim to acknowledge Jesus' atonement as evidence of divine love unifying man and God through Christ Jesus, who they refer to as the "Way-shower"; and that man is saved through Christ, through Truth, Life, and Love as demonstrated by the "Galilean Prophet" in healing the sick and overcoming sin and death. However, Jesus is not God, and therefore, not perfect. Biblically, we are told that the only reason God will allow Jesus to be our atonement and sacrifice, is because He is the perfect, sinless, unblemished lamb. 1 Peter 1:19, Hebrews 9:11-22.

*She (Eddy) says that the crucifixion of Jesus

and His resurrection served to uplift faith, and to understand eternal life, even the 'all ness' of Soul and Spirit, and the 'nothing nesses' of matter (as Christian Science is based on a premise that nothing surrounding us actually exists but is only in our minds. That all matter is simply an illusion). According to Christian Science, the ordinary materialist view of man and the universe provides a false sense of reality that is the inadequacy of human perception. Eddy argued that the traditional Christian belief that matter is created by God is a fallacy that leads to the conclusion that God is responsible for all suffering in the universe and that salvation involves the resurrection of "the flesh". Beginning in Genesis 1, the Bible tells a very different story about creation, matter and who brought everything into being.

She relates that redemption from sin is basic to salvation because sin in all its forms is a denial of God's sovereignty predicated on the belief that life, will and mind evolve from matter rather than from spirit. At the same time Eddy, unlike some of her more optimistic followers, saw redemption as a very long and demanding process of self-reflection, calling upon the Christian virtues of patience, humility, repentance and cross-bearing. The Christian Bible reminds us over and over that redemption is only through God's Grace, by Jesus' blood, Ephesians 1:7, Colossians 1:20-22.

*Eddy's view of the material world and practices stemming from it distinguished Christian Science from similar movements of the time. While she shared some thoughts with the followers of philosophical idealism (which also stresses the role of spirit versus matter in understanding the world), especially concerning transcendentalism, her emphasis on healing differentiates Christian Science from forms of idealism that sort out experiences but do not attempt to affect them. In Christian Science the cure of disease through prayer is seen as a very necessary element in the process of redemption. Eddy's teachings have led to a complex relationship between church members and the medical establishment, even leading to court proceedings to protect children of practicing members. Church members are, instead, prompted to pray for healing, or to seek out one of the denomination's Christian Science Practitioners, to pray for them, who are listed in a directory that is published monthly in the church's periodical. Practitioners usually charge their patients a nominal fee.

*Eddy's rejection of the divine creation of matter most clearly differentiates Christian Science from traditional Christianity, in which God's creation of the universe and the incarnation of Jesus are core beliefs. Christian leaders have noted that although Eddy used some Christian language in setting up her belief system, she did so to create a completely different religion.

*I think it is clear we are not praying to the same god.

Jehovah's Witness

*Jehovah's Witnesses do believe in God the Father (whose Name is Jehovah). However, to their way of thinking Jesus Christ, though being

God's firstborn Son, is inferior to God and was created by God. They also believe that the Holy Spirit is not a person, but merely God's active force. When comparing these beliefs to Bible scripture we find many discrepancies, so let us begin at the beginning.

*Jehovah's Witnesses claim that God has only one name. Yet the Bible gives us many: 'God, or in Hebrew 'Elohim' (Genesis 1:1); God Almighty, or in Hebrew 'El Shadday' (Genesis 17:1); Lord, or in Hebrew 'Adonay' (Psalm 8:1); and Lord of Hosts, or in Hebrew 'yhwhtseba'ot' (from 1 Samuel 1), among others. In the New Testament Jesus refers to God as Father, (Matthew 6:9), as did the apostles (1 Corinthians 1:3). We can clearly see that Jehovah is not the only Name by which we know God.

*Jehovah's Witnesses say that they accept the entire Bible but are not 'fundamentalists' and that they recognize parts of the Bible are written in figurative, or symbolic, language and 'should not be understood as written'. They claim their belief system and practice is made up of the 'raw material' of the Bible but is done so without predetermining what was to be found there. This leaves much to their own interpretation, as we find when we examine individual items of their system of beliefs.

*Jehovah's Witnesses believe the Trinity to be unbiblical, because the word 'Trinity' does not appear in the Bible. However, though 'Trinity' is a manmade word, we use it to represent the 'triune' nature of one God in three persons. While it is true that there is only one God, three persons are called God in Scripture: The Father (1 Peter 1:2); Jesus (John 20:28, Hebrews 1:8) and the Holy Spirit (Acts 5:3-4).

Each of these possesses the attributes of deity – including omnipresence (Psalms 139:7, Jeremiah 23:23-24, Matthew 28:20); omniscience (Psalms 147:5, John 16:30, 1 Corinthians 2:10-11); omnipotence (Jeremiah 32:17, John 2:1-11, Romans 15:19); and eternality (Psalms 90:2, Hebrews 9:14, Revelation 22:13).

Additionally, each of the three is involved in the workings of deity, such as creating the universe: The Father (Genesis 1:1, Psalms 102:25); the Son (John 1:3, Colossians 1:16, Hebrews 1:2); and the Holy Spirit (Genesis 1:2, Job 33:4, Psalms 104:30). The Bible clearly indicates that there is 'three-in-oneness' in the godhead (Matthew 28:19, 2 Corinthians 13:14). Therefore, doctrinal support for using the word 'Trinity' is compellingly strong.

Understanding the Trinity may be impossible but proving that the Trinity is scriptural is not an especially difficult task. If we simply define the Trinity accurately and show that the Bible distinctly teaches the details of that definition, it makes no difference whether the word "Trinity" appears in the text or not. What matters is that the doctrine of a triune God is taught there.

*On the matter of Jesus and His equality with God. Jehovah's Witnesses believe that Jesus was created by Jehovah first as the archangel Michael before the physical world existed and though He is 'a' god, He is a lesser god.

Biblically, however, Jesus is eternally God

(John 1:1, 8:58, Exodus 3:14) and has the exact same divine nature as the Father (John 5:18, 10:30, Hebrews 1:3). If we compare Old Testament and New Testament, we see that scripture equates Jesus and Jehovah (compare Isaiah 43:11 with Titus 2:13; Isaiah 44:24 with Colossians 1:16; and Isaiah 6:1-5 with John 12:41).

We can see through further study that Jesus could not be an angel, because He Himself created the angels (Colossians 1:16, John 1:3, Hebrews 1:2-10) and is worshiped by them (Hebrews 1:6).

*Jehovah's Witnesses believe that when Jesus was born on earth, He was a mere human and not God in human flesh. This violates the Biblical teaching that in the incarnate Jesus, "the whole fullness of deity dwells bodily" (Colossians

2:9, Philippians 2:6-7). The Greek word for "fullness" (pleroma) carries the idea of the sum total. "Deity" (theotes, in Greek) refers to the nature, being and attributes of God. Therefore, the incarnate Jesus was the sum total of the nature, being and attributes of God in bodily form. Indeed, Jesus is Immanuel, or "God with us" (Matthew 1:23, Isaiah 7:14, John 1:1, 14, 18, 10:30, 14:9-10).

*Jehovah's Witnesses believe that Jesus was resurrected spiritually from the dead, but not physically. Biblically, the resurrected Jesus asserted that He was not merely a spirit but had a flesh-and-bone body (Luke 24:39, John 2:19-21).

He ate food, after His resurrection, on several occasions. Thereby proving he had a genuine physical body after being raised from the dead on the third day (Luke 24:30, John 21:12-13). These things were confirmed by His followers, who physically touched Him (Matthew 28:9, John 20:17).

*Jehovah's Witnesses believe that the second coming has already occurred. That it was an invisible, spiritual event which took place in the year 1914. Biblically, however, the yet-future second coming will be physical, visible and will be accompanied by visible cosmic disturbances (Acts 1:9-11, Titus 2:13, Matthew 24:29-30. Every eye will see Him (Revelation 1:7).

*Jehovah's Witnesses believe the Holy Spirit is an impersonal force of God and not a distinct person. Yet the Bible says the Holy Spirit has the three primary attributes of personality: a mind (Romans 8:27), emotions (Ephesians

4:30), and a will (1Corinthians 12:11). Personal pronouns are used of the Holy Spirit (Acts 13:2). Additionally, He does things that only a person can do, including teaching (John 14:26), testifying (John 15:26), commissioning (Acts 13:4), issuing commands (Acts 8:29), and interceding (Romans 8:26). The Holy Spirit is clearly the third person of the Trinity, as seen in (Matthew 28:19).

*Jehovah's Witnesses believe there are 'two distinct groups of people who will be redeemed' and that these two groups have a very different end story. The first is the Anointed Class of 144,000 who will live in heaven and rule with Christ. The second class is referred to as the "other sheep" (all other believers) who will live on an earthly paradise. Biblically, however, a heavenly destiny awaits ALL who believe in Christ and ask Him to come into their hearts as Lord and Savior (John 14:1-3, 17:24, 2Corinthians 5:1, Philippians 3:20, Colossians 1:5, 1Thess. 4:7, Hebrews 3:1). We are also told that ALL these people will dwell on the new earth (2Peter 3:13, Revelation 21:1-4).

*Jehovah's Witnesses believe hell is not a place of eternal suffering but is rather the common grave of humankind. The wicked are annihilated – snuffed out of conscious existence forever. Scripturally hell is a real place of conscious, eternal suffering. (Matthew 5:22, 25:41, 46, Jude 7, Revelation 14:11, 20:10, 14).

*Most importantly, Jehovah's Witnesses believe that salvation requires faith in Christ in association with God's organization (which is their religion) and includes firm obedience to its rules. Biblically, viewing obedience to rules as a requirement for salvation nullifies the Gospel message (Galatians 2:16-21, Colossians 2:20-23). Salvation is based only and wholly on God's unmerited favor (grace), not on the believer's performance or affiliations.

I believe there is more than sufficient evidence here to suggest that we are not praying to the same god, but feel free to come to your own conclusion.

Are we praying to the same God?

I believe there is ample proof in the preceding examples to suggest that many of these religions and denominations are praying to gods of their own making. Ones who do not line up to the

Christian Biblical God, but with their own idea of a god who suits their individual purposes. As Christians we do not have the luxury of inventing a god to fit into the slot we have created for his existence. God is God. He is the creator. The beginning and the end, whose Name is Jesus. We don't get to go about inventing the truth, as Truth already exists in the entirety of Jesus Christ. We don't get to follow the rules that please us and ignore the ones that don't. And yes, sometimes the things we read in the Bible are difficult. However, God's plans are for our best. Plans for good and not for evil.

As I said previously, I am not writing, "God?" to disparage another's religion or culture. Each of us must decide in our own hearts and minds the way which gives us most peace, even if that decision ultimately takes us on a path that leads away from the Lord (though I can't imagine true peace anywhere else). This is called freedom of choice. However, all this evidence causes me (and perhaps some of you) to beg the question, "Why, with all of the substantiation to the contrary, do many in the world try to convince us that we are all praying to the same god?"

Simply, there is an agenda involved. Through extensive research I have discovered that this trend of persons trying hard to convince us that we all pray to the same god has been going on for centuries. I wondered why and saw that at least in the nineteenth, twentieth, and twenty-first centuries many of the pushes in that direction have coincided with other events or leaders of the age urging society toward a one world government. When researching those events and individuals I discovered a disturbing trend. That trend is globalism.

With all the shouting going on about Democrats and Republicans we sometimes forget there are other forces at work in the world. Forces much more frightening and heinous than any political party. While it is true that globalists may be using far left and far right proponents to achieve many of their goals, this is a vastly more far-reaching movement than left or right and is obviously headed up by the one who would rip us from our Savior's arms, if indeed he were able, Satan.

Are we praying to the same God? If we are Christians, which means, literally, (little Christs, or followers of Christ), then Jesus must be the answer. If your religion or denomination tells you in its writings, creeds or manmade rules that there is any way to Father God, or salvation, other than through Jesus and Jesus alone; or proposes that you must do anything of yourself for that salvation, then you should pick up your Bible and begin doing some research. I would start here, in Romans 10:9 "Because, if you confess with your mouth that Jesus is Lord and believe in your heart that God raised Him from the dead, you will be saved."

God loves you. He has given you a way to come to Him. One way. It must be done of your own free will and we must use the commonsense God has given us in conjunction with the Word of God to determine if that way is of Him. In every case, examine how the words of that path match up to the Word He has given us to follow. 1 John 4:1-4 "Beloved, do not believe every spirit, but test the spirits to see whether they are from God, for many false prophets have gone out into the world. By this you know the Spirit of God: every spirit that confesses that Jesus Christ has come in the flesh is from God, and every spirit that does not confess Jesus is not from God. This is the spirit of the antichrist, which you heard was coming and now is in the world already. Little children, you are from God and have overcome them, for He who is in you is greater than he who is in the world."

Why Do Bad Things Happen to Good People?

This is a good question and one we have heard more times than we can count. Along with similar questions, such as, "If your God is so good, how can He let things like this happen?" and "How can you claim that God loves us when my Dad, Mom, sister, brother, child.......or everything we own, etc., is sick, broken or gone?"

As a matter of fact, I wondered about the goodness of God for quite a while when my eight-month-old baby was taken by S.I.D.S. many years ago.

Personally, and I suppose when all is said and

done, thankfully, I have never suffered from any illusions that I was a "good" person, as I have done many stupid and thoughtless things in my life, and many unspeakable things were done to me as a child and a young woman.

After much thought, I guess I simply concluded that God didn't want me to raise this precious baby boy due to the inherent evil in my own soul. So, I continued with my life, in the same mindset I'd held as irrefutable truth throughout childhood. That frame of mind being that I was the single most unworthy and unlovable human being on the planet earth.

However, though I personally suffered most of my life from a mindset of total unworthiness, I've also met many individuals who believe they are inherently good and not sinful, completely on their own, and do not "deserve" any of the evil that befalls them.

So, first let's address the issue of "goodness".

Since the fall of Adam in the garden mankind has been drowning in sin. No human is inherently good on his/her own. I'm not saying that we don't do good things on occasion (some more than others), however, our goodness (and therefore our worthiness to be blessed) is not dependent on our own actions, but on the ultimate sacrifice of Jesus Christ and His undying love for us. All our sin, if we have believed on Him, is covered by His blood (not to say that we should go about committing sin just because we know we are saved, that is ridiculous and very unproductive). The Bible makes it clear that we are not capable of the kind of goodness needed to achieve salvation, or indeed in order to achieve a pain free and blessed life on our own. Even Jesus didn't consider Himself good apart from God. See Mark 10:18 "And Jesus said to him, "Why do you call me good? No one is good except God alone."

No. Please understand that mankind without Christ is thoroughly wicked. Apart from Jesus there is no good in us at all. 1 John 1:8-10 says, "If we say we have no sin, we deceive ourselves, and the truth is not in us. If we confess our sins, He is faithful and just to forgive us our sins and to cleanse us from all unrighteousness. If we say we have not sinned, we make Him a liar and His Word is not in us." Also, Mark 7:21-23, "For from within, out of the heart of man, come evil thoughts, sexual immorality, theft, murder, adultery, coveting, wickedness, deceit, sensuality, envy, slander, pride, foolishness. All these evil things come from within, and they defile a person."

None of us 'deserves' God's blessings, or His Grace and mercy, for we all fall short of the glory of God. But He, out of His boundless love, gives to us abundantly when we confess our need of a Savior, give our hearts to Him and ask Him to be our Lord.

When I was young, I wondered why so many people had so much more than I did. My question wasn't so much, "Why do bad things happen to good people?", but rather, "Why do so many good things happen to people who are so obviously bad and wicked?". As a young woman I was very confused by the disparity in wealth and means of those around me. After all, I worked hard, I took care of my kids, I was honest (well mostly), so why didn't I see the results that others were seeing. I knew many people who were evil to the core. People who hurt me. People who cheated and did other terrible things. Yet those people were successful, with good standing in the community and much wealth.

Again, I assumed God was punishing me for the wickedness in my own journey. I didn't understand that this was simply part of life. I didn't realize then that bad things happen to everyone and, conversely, good things happen to everyone (though it may not feel like that sometimes). Read Matthew 5:43-45 "You have heard that it was said, 'you shall love your neighbor and hate your enemy'. But I say to you, 'Love your enemies and pray for those who persecute you, so that you may be sons of your Father who is in heaven. For He makes His sun rise on the evil and on the good and sends rain on the just and on the unjust."

Then, in October of 2010 I was diagnosed with stage 4 breast cancer, which had metastasized in six other locations in my body and I was told I had three to six months to live. I was completely floored and pretty sure I was already dead (that is, if it depended on my own worthiness to live). I looked back over my life and realized I'd never done anything of significance to bring God glory. I was truly ashamed by that realization.

Now, the strange thing was that at this juncture of my life, I was also the pastor's wife and had read the Bible dozens and dozens of times in those twenty years (now 30) of marriage to my husband as he ministered to various churches in the area.

However, though I'd read the Bible over and over. The Words, His Words, had never made it past my flawed, mortal vision and into the eyes and heart of my spirit. Due to the horrors of my childhood and my youth I was convinced that God had no time for me. That is, until I was forced to make time, real time, for Him, sitting alone at my kitchen table as I awaited my fate.

I was being treated with many different drugs and successive rounds of radiation, which were making me sick and keeping me from doing the things I would ordinarily do. I was at the cancer center so many days of the week at this point that I ultimately lost my job as office manager of a large church. So, I sat, fearful, dejected and alone, with my Bible.

I began to study. I reviewed scriptures I'd read many times before. Verses that previously had not made it past my brain matter and into my heart. Scriptures that began to give me real hope. I discovered many surprising and wonderful healing pieces of God's Word. Hope filled verses that I copied onto page after page of loose-leaf paper and began reading, out loud, in the middle of my kitchen three times a day.

To make a long story short (one you can read in my first book, "When All Else Fails, God's Grace and the Power of Prayer), over a period of time I came to trust the Lord for healing. A healing I now understood had already been paid for over two thousand years ago on Calvary.

Through His Grace I was completely healed of cancer and of the debilitating hopelessness that had formerly enveloped me.

I wrote my first book while I was going through treatments and then began to speak at churches and women's groups around the area. At one of those meetings a woman came up to me and demanded to know what the heck I thought made me so special. She asked why God would heal me and not her beloved mother. She was quite angry and accusatory. I tried to explain to her that my healing had nothing to do with me. I explained that I really wasn't anything special at all on my own and that only through Jesus' righteousness could I claim to be righteous at all. 2 Corinthians 5:21 "For our sake He made Him to be sin who knew no sin, so that in Him we might become the righteousness of God."

I told her all I knew was that I'd been healed by the sacrifice Jesus already made on the cross. She seemed to be very incensed at this and stomped away, mad at God, or mad at me, I'm not sure.

Throughout this process of getting to know my Savior, one which has included eleven surgeries in ten years, (some of us take longer to get the important stuff than others), my zeal for the Lord and His Word has only grown more powerful. However, I have encountered other situations in my life and the lives of those I love that have required much additional prayer. Prayer is powerful. Prayer works. Some of these needs have been met with instantaneous and miraculous healing, some were healed over a longer period and for others we are still awaiting the physical manifestation of those results.

I can't explain why some are healed and others are not. Perhaps, in some cases, a time will come in that unhealed person's life when the miracle of their healing would help to bring another to salvation. John 9:1-3, "As He passed by, He saw a man blind from birth. And His disciples asked Him, Rabbi, who sinned, this man or his parents, that he was born blind?" Jesus answered, "It was not that this man sinned, or his parents, but that the works of God might be displayed in him."

An illness might even be that thorn in our side, as in the example Paul, necessary for God's will to come to fruition. Look at 2Corinthians 12:7-9, "So to keep me from becoming conceited because of the surpassing greatness of the revelations, a thorn was given me in the flesh, a messenger of

Satan to harass me, to keep me from becoming conceited. Three times I pleaded with the Lord about this, that it should leave me. But He said to me, "My grace is sufficient for you, for My power is made perfect in weakness."

I know, now, without a single doubt, that God wants only the best for me. He will use anything the enemy throws at me for my good and His purposes. He will do the same for you.

When there is something I should learn, God will use a circumstance in my life to show me His will, or to impart an important lesson for which I'm in need. I have learned that nothing is ever wasted in God's Kingdom. I have grown to be more patient (most of the time) with God's timing, something which has taken a great deal of His help to accomplish. I've learned to understand that the enemy (Satan) comes only to kill, steal and destroy and that God (who is my truest friend and rescuer), is still on the throne.

So, when Satan comes against me with mischief or destruction of any kind, to commit "bad" against me or those I love, I set my mind to prayer and wait for the Lord to come to my rescue and make things right. I know this to be the correct path, because Romans 8:28 tells me, "And we know that for those who love God all things work together for good for those who are called according to His purpose."

The real question, then, isn't, "Why do bad things happen to good people?" or "Why do nice things happen to bad people?" The real question is, do you trust the Lord to see you through anything the enemy throws at you. Remembering that He always has your best interests in mind. Get to know God's Word. Store it in your heart and mind and whenever Satan comes against you or those you love; you will have all the ammunition you need to defeat him.

Also, please remember to share the love and grace of Jesus with your loved ones and with all those that God chooses to place in your path. Once they are covered by the blood of Christ, you don't have to wonder about their eternal destination. If something in this world should take them from this place you will know they have a home with the Father, and you will see them again. There is no greater comfort than that found in the arms of the Lord.

Why Does God Allow Suffering?

Wildfires burning out of control in the West. Hurricanes, tornadoes, floods and earthquakes striking with unprecedented frequency and terrorist attacks around the world at an all-time high. Now, add to that, dealing with a pandemic that has shut down society as we know it. Those events on top of the everyday pain and suffering going on in individual's lives—maybe even yours—has people asking questions.

Where there is illness, sorrow, injuries, abuse, betrayal, broken relationships, disappointment, heartache, crime and death, you might be wondering why?

In the Bible we see accounts from Job, and the writers of the Psalms and we discover that this question has been asked throughout the ages by many who are encountering pain in their own lives.

During the 20th century we witnessed two World Wars, the Holocaust, devastating famines in Africa, genocides in China and the Soviet Union, the killing fields of Cambodia, the genocide in Rwanda, the emergence of AIDS and the ethnic cleansing of Kosovo. Along came the 21st century with 9/11 and the Syrian slaughters among other things. The list goes on and on. Will we ever forget 2020? I doubt it.

A national survey was commissioned several years ago. In the survey respondents answered one question, "If they could ask God one question, what would that question be?" The number one response was, "Why is there suffering in the world?"

I have a friend who led a life of relative peace and prosperity. She was married to a great guy, had healthy children and was deeply loved from childhood onward (in fact a bit spoiled by her parents and then her husband) her whole life. She never wanted for anything and never had to answer the tough questions brought on by turmoil. She went to church every Sunday and lived her life wondering why some people asked that question, "Why is there suffering in the world?"

You see, suffering had never touched her, or her household, so she wasn't affected by its random glancing blows. She spent a considerable amount of time, though, admonishing others to keep their chins up and remain in faith when tragedy befell them; commenting behind their backs, to others, that she was particularly annoyed by their whining. "Why was their faith not stronger?" She asked.

Then, she and her family were struck by a series of tragic events, the death of first her father and then her brother. Soon after, her husband contracted a terrible disease and languished for several years before meeting a sad and horrific end. She was angry and bitter. She learned the hard way why it was that people asked that question. No matter how hard I tried, she would not be consoled and suddenly she was that person asking why there was suffering in the world.

There are very few people in this world who

have not encountered their own share of tragedies. My friend was a rare exception. So, I'm not altogether sure why people are so surprised when suffering strikes. Unlike religious leaders who write off pain and suffering as illusions, Jesus was blunt and truthful with His followers. He said in John 16:33, "You will have suffering in this world." He didn't say you might have suffering, He said it is absolutely going to happen.

Obviously, I cannot stand in God's shoes, so to speak, and give a complete answer to that question. I don't have God's mind. I don't see with His eyes. What a blessing and a curse that would be, huh? 1 Corinthians 13:12 says, "For now we see in a mirror dimly, but then face to face. Now I know in part; then I shall know fully, even as I have been fully known." For now, everything that I see is partial and incomplete and when asked this question my response must be, "I don't know. I just don't know why there is suffering in the world."

What I do know is that we live in a fallen world, a world crippled by sin. That sin, this broken world, is caused by man's downfall not the downfall of God. I also know that if we follow Him and allow our lives to be directed by Him, we will finally be headed in the right direction.

I've often heard, "If God is such a loving God, why didn't He just create a world where tragedy and suffering didn't exist?" The answer to that question is: He did! Genesis 1:31 says, "God saw all that He had made, and it was very good."

So, if God is not the author of tragedy and wickedness, where did these things come from?

Well, God has existed throughout eternity as the Father, Son and Spirit, together in a relationship of perfect love and unity, so, love is of the highest value in the universe. When He decided to create human beings, He wanted us to be able to experience love, to love one another and to love Him. However, to give us the ability to love, He also had to give us free will to decide whether to love or not to love. Why? Because love always involves a choice.

If we were merely programmed to say, "I love you", it wouldn't be love, but only meaningless words. When my granddaughter was small, we bought her a doll. The doll had a string in her back that when pulled made the doll say, "I love you". So, did that plastic doll love my granddaughter? Of course, not. The doll was a toy, merely programmed to say those words.

To really experience love the doll would have needed to be able to choose to love or not to love. As I said, real love always involves a choice. Just like the choice our Heavenly Father made to come to earth as a human being and to die on the cross for us to free us from sin and the grave; and just like the choice we must make to follow, or not follow the Savior.

For us to experience real love, God gave us free will. Unfortunately, humans have abused our free will by rejecting God and walking away from Him. In the garden, when man decided he wanted to be his own God, humanity began a spiral into wickedness that would introduce both moral and natural evil into the perfect world God had created for us as a habitation.

Due to this we often make choices that are selfish, arrogant, uncaring, hateful or abusive. Romans 3:23 tells us that, "All have sinned and fall short of the glory of God."

Much of our world's suffering is simply a result of our own sinful action, or inaction. For example, people look at famine that cripples much of the world and they ask, "Where is God?", but did you know that our planet produces enough food for every man, woman and child to have 3000 calories a day? It is our responsibility to see that the food is distributed, so that we don't have children around the world starving on our watch. If you can't be there to do it yourself, there are organizations around the world who will gladly accept your donation to see that the problem is addressed. It is our own self-centeredness that keeps people from being fed. This is moral evil.

Through Christ we are to be the servant hands and feet of God on earth. It's up to us how we choose to use those hands and feet. You can use your hand to hold a gun and shoot someone, or to feed the hungry, but it is unfair to shoot someone and then blame God for the existence of suffering. Only in a morally bankrupt mind does that make sense.

Natural evils are those things like earthquakes, wildfires, hurricanes, tornadoes and plagues that cause suffering for people. These too are the indirect result of sin in the world. When we humans told God to get lost, He partially honored our request. He won't force Himself on you after all. When that happened nature began to revolt. The earth was cursed. Genetic breakdown and disease began. Pain and death became part of the human experience.

The Bible makes it clear that it is because of sin that nature is corrupt. This is when "thorns and thistles" entered the world. Romans 8:22 says, "We know that the whole creation has been groaning as in the pains of childbirth right up to the present time." This means that even nature longs for redemption to come and for the source of all the disorder and chaos in the world to be set right.

Many will ask, "Didn't God foresee all of this suffering?" I don't doubt that He did. He is Omniscient. But look at it this way: If you are a parent, even before you had children, didn't you know that there was a possibility they might suffer disappointment, pain and heartache in life; or even that they might be badly hurt, or walk away from you never to be seen again? Of course, you did, but you still had kids anyway, didn't you? Why? Because even though you knew that in giving them life there would be a potential for great pain and suffering, there was also the equally great possibility of joy and deep love. A life of great meaning.

I realize this analogy is not perfect but think about God. He knew we would rebel against Him, but He also knew many would choose to follow Him, have a loving relationship with Him, and spend eternity with Him in Heaven. It was all worth it to Him, even though it would cost His own beloved Son pain and suffering we could never imagine in order to achieve their redemption.

It helps me, as I ponder the mystery of pain and suffering, to remember that God did not create them, but rather man in His vain grab for glory birthed this mess. I have discovered that I tend to grow far more in my faith and in my relationship with Him when I am going through the storms of life rather than the moments of calm, you know, valleys and mountaintops, so I tend these days to look for the good to come when times are rocky.

I have also discovered that though suffering and pain never feel good, God can always use them to bring about good. He does this by keeping His promise that goes, "And we know that in all things God works for the good of those who love Him, who have been called according to His purpose." Romans 8:28.

You will note that the verse does not say that God causes the suffering, just that He promises to cause good to emerge from it. The verse also does not say that we will immediately, or even in this life, see what good God caused to come from that time of pain and suffering. Remember, we only see things dimly in this world. I also want you to notice that God doesn't make this promise, of Romans 8:28, to everyone. His pledge to take a bad circumstance and use it for good is made to those who follow Him. Those who give their lives to Jesus and make Him the Lord of their lives. So, if you know of someone who is suffering and wondering why God is allowing their pain, you might share His saving grace and explain to them that He takes care of His children.

I love the story of Joseph in the Old Testament.

Sold into slavery by his own brothers, unfairly accused of a crime and falsely imprisoned. Finally, after a dozen years, he was placed in a role of great authority where he was able to save the lives of his family and many others. This is what he said to his brothers in Genesis 50:20, "As for you, you meant evil against me, but God meant it for good, to bring it about that many people should be kept alive, as they are today."

If you are committed to God, He promises that He can and will take whatever pain you are experiencing; whatever suffering surrounds your circumstances and draw something good from it.

Maybe you don't believe me? You might be thinking, "No, there has been too much pain in my life, too much damage done, too much suffering. There is no way He can turn things around and cause good to come from this mess."

But if you doubt God's promise, remember this, He took the absolute worst thing that ever happened in the history of the universe, the death of Jesus on the cross, and turned it into the best thing that ever happened in the history of the universe. He opened heaven to every person who would follow Him. So, if He can take the worst possible moment in history and turn it into the best, He can certainly take your worst circumstances and create something good.

I used to wonder what "good" He might draw from the negative things I had endured, until I realized how He was using my circumstances to mold and sharpen my own character, to influence others for Him, to draw unbelievers in and to strengthen my own faith. Now I see the lives

He has touched through my experiences and I am blessed.

I have often heard people say, "If God has the power to rid the world of evil and suffering, then why doesn't He do it?"

To that I will say, just because He hasn't done it yet, doesn't mean He won't do it. Well, the story isn't over yet, is it?

The Bible tells us the day will come when sickness and pain will be eradicated and people who have not trusted Jesus for salvation will be held accountable for the evil they've committed. Justice will be served. That day is coming, but not yet.

So, what the heck is taking Him so long? What's holding Him up? The answer to that is that He is delaying the consummation of history in hopes that some of you who have not put your trust in Jesus will decide to do that before it is too late. He is waiting for you because He loves you and doesn't want you to be left behind to suffer. 2Peter 3:9 tells us, "The Lord is not slow in keeping His promise, as some understand slowness. He is patient with you, not wanting anyone to perish, but everyone to come to repentance." What a loving God!

I would never want to minimize anyone's pain and suffering. I haven't walked a mile in your shoes. However, sometimes it benefits us to look at things from a long-term perspective. I want you to read the following verse, understanding it was written by Paul, who suffered through beatings, stoning and shipwrecks, as well as unjust imprisonments, rejections, hunger, thirst and homelessness. Far more pain than I've endured in my lifetime. 2Corinthians 4:17, "For this light momentary affliction is preparing for us and eternal weight of glory Beyond all comparison."

He also wrote in Romans 8:18, "For I consider that the sufferings of this present time are not worth comparing with the glory that is to be revealed to us."

Listen, I'm not making light of the suffering you or anyone has endured in your lifetime here, however long or short. I am simply reminding you that in the larger scheme of things, when we look at the endless joy, we, who have trusted in the Lord, will experience in paradise with The King, we will likely look back and admit that no negative thing we have endured could dampen the wondrous happiness we will experience with Him.

It's like a story I heard once. A British church leader, Galvin Reid, met a young man who had fallen down a flight of stairs when he was just a baby and shattered his back. He'd been in and out of hospitals, surgery after surgery his whole life, yet he made the astounding comment that he thinks God is fair. Reid asked him, "How old are you?" The boy said, "Seventeen." Reid asked, "How many years have you spent in hospitals?" the boy said, "Thirteen years." The pastor exclaimed, "And you think that's fair?" The boy replied, "Well, God has all eternity to make it up to me."

And He will! God promises us a time when there will be no more crying, no more pain and suffering. A time when we'll be joined with God in perfect harmony, forever. Read this breathtaking verse in Corinthians 2:9 and let your soul absorb the words, "No eye has seen, no ear has heard, no mind has conceived what God has prepared for those who love Him."

Every one of us has seen examples of how the same suffering causes one person to turn bitter, hard and angry, and to reject God. While another suffering soul turns to God, becoming gentler, loving and tender. Willing to use their own pain to make another's life easier. Examples abound, such as one who loses a child to a drunk driver, giving in to chronic rage and endless despair, while another reaches out by founding Mothers Against Drunk Drivers.

In our pain and suffering we make the choice to run away from God or run toward Him. Not everyone will learn, and therefore benefit, from their suffering, because that part is up to us. It's our free will. We can be victims, or victors.

Clear back at the start of my answer, I quoted the beginning of John 16:33, now let me give you the entire verse, "I have told you these things so that in me you may have peace. You will have suffering in this world. But be courageous! I have conquered the world." Suffering doesn't have the last word anymore. God has the last word!

Why Must I Forgive?

Silly, but I am always the first one to tell on myself. I figure its better this way, though, because things have a way of coming out, and me admitting I'm a jerk is better than someone else doing it.

I spent many years angry at people who'd hurt me when I was a child and then at others who hurt me and misused me when I was a young woman. So, understanding the emotional logic and spiritual perspective of forgiveness was an epiphany I refused to embrace for quite some time. It was extremely hard to let go of the hate, even as it ate me up from the inside out.

However, when I came to the realization that the only person who is being wounded by that hate and a refusal to forgive is the one who won't forgive, I finally gave in. Laying all that hostility and anger at the foot of the cross allowed the mending to begin. Forgiveness was a healing balm that slowly erased every bit of the hate and anger I had bottled up for so long. Now, all I want is to introduce the world to Jesus and to share that restoration power with everyone I meet.

Haven't we all been in situations where someone, maybe even a person we trusted, has dealt us a blow? Perhaps not physically, but emotionally, or even financially. When you feel taken advantage of, or this person's actions have created a problem that has damaged some facet of your life, it's hard to let it go and forgive. When you must dig deep inside to find even the remotest desire to offer forgiveness, (with no strings attached), it's hard. However, if you ask the Lord to help you find that desire, He will help you. He is an expert on the whole grace and mercy thing after all.

We've also, every one of us, been in circumstances where we have done wrong to someone else and desire forgiveness – from a spouse, family member, friend, or even a co-worker. Heck, sometimes the person we most need forgiveness from is ourselves.

Whether you are the one giving or receiving forgiveness it is a very powerful thing, a thing that can change your heart.

The most important thing to know about forgiveness is that God wants us to forgive, to forgive as we have been forgiven. The Scriptures are filled with wonderful words that encourage us to, and even demand for us to forgive. I have included a few:

Ephesians 4:32, "Be kind and compassionate to one another, forgiving each other, just as in Christ God forgave you."

Matthew 6:14, "For is you forgive other people when they sin against you, your heavenly Father will also forgive you."

Colossians 3:13, "Bear with each other and forgive one another if any of you has a grievance against someone. Forgive as the Lord forgave you."

Luke 6:37, "Do not judge and you will not be judged. Do not condemn and you will not be condemned. Forgive and you will be forgiven."

Matthew 18:21-22, "Then Peter came to Jesus and asked, 'Lord, how many times shall I forgive my brother or sister who sins against me. Up to seven times?' Jesus answered, 'I tell you, not seven times, but seventy-seven times.'"

Psalm 86:5, "You, Lord, are forgiving and good, abounding in love to all who call to you."

Mark 11:25, "And when you stand praying, if you hold anything against anyone, forgive them, so that your Father in heaven may forgive you your sins."

Psalm 32:1, "Blessed is the one whose transgressions are forgiven, whose sins are covered."

Matthew 6:15, "But if you do not forgive others their sins, your Father will not forgive your sins."

1John 1:9, "If we confess our sins, He is faithful and just to forgive us our sins and to cleanse us from all unrighteousness."

Hebrews 8:12, "For I will forgive their

wickedness and will remember their sins no more."

Proverbs 17:9, "Love prospers when a fault is forgiven, but dwelling on it separates close friends."

Isaiah 43:25, "I, even I, am He who blots out your transgressions, for My own sake, and remembers your sins no more."

Ephesians 1:7-8, "In Him we have redemption through His blood, the forgiveness of sins, according to the riches of His grace which He made to abound toward us in all wisdom and prudence."

Colossians 1:13-14, "He has delivered us from the power of darkness and conveyed us into the kingdom of the Son of His love, in whom we have redemption through His blood, the redemption of sins."

Does God Still Perform Healings and Other Miracles?

This is an easy one for me. I am living proof that God still heals.

Going through a time of healing, whether it is physical, emotional, or spiritual, can be very difficult. Sometimes we can feel as if we are facing these challenges alone, even if we have family and friends as a support system.

When the healing isn't immediate, or after a period doesn't seem to be coming at all, we might conclude that we didn't deserve God's healing, or worse, that He just doesn't care.

Let me assure you, He does care. But, let's be

honest, none of us "deserves" His healing. God loves us and blesses us out of His abundance, due to the suffering and sacrifice of His Son, Jesus, not as payment for who we are, or for anything we've done. We can't earn our miracles and blessings any more than we can earn our salvation. We can never be "good enough" on our own. Jesus suffered and died for our healing and peace of mind. Isaiah 53:5 "But He was wounded for our transgressions; He was crushed for our iniquities; upon Him was the chastisement that brought us peace, and with His stripes we are healed."

Better than that. Jesus died not only for our sins, but for our total healing, body, soul and spirit, over two thousand years ago and His promise of healing is every bit as valid today as it was then! 1 Peter 2:24 says, "He Himself bore our sins in His body on the tree, that we might die to sin and live to righteousness. By His wounds you have been healed." Notice it says, "You have been healed." Not that you might be, or that this is a future incident down the road. Have been is a past event. Your healing has already taken place. It took place on the cross and you must trust the Lord that it is yours and available to you in this moment of time. Accept that healing and believe it without wavering, until you see the physical results manifesting.

I have heard from some that miracles, like healing, were only for the apostolic age. However, I don't find any Biblical proof that our God has changed. Numbers 23:19, "God is not man, that He should lie, or a son of man, that He should change His mind. Has He said, and will He not do it? Or has He spoken, and will not fulfill it?" Or in Hebrews 13:8, "Jesus Christ is the same yesterday and today and forever." No, He has not changed. Our God is still firmly in the miracle working business.

I would add that God can use anything we face in our lives to help us, or others, to grow spiritually. Whether you know Christ as Savior or not, He knows the number of your days and where you will be when you leave this earthly plain, heaven or hell. I can't think of anywhere in the universe I'd rather be than in the arms of Jesus. The time to decide about your eternal destiny is now.

Perhaps there are others in your realm of influence who do not know the Lord as Savior? He knows that too. Might they be persuaded to believe on Christ Jesus by your circumstances, or your firm and abiding faith through difficult situations? God knows that as well. He doesn't want anyone to be left behind and He will use the trials in your life to reach those unsaved among us if you will let Him do so. In 2 Peter 3:9 we read, "The Lord is not slow to fulfill His promise as some count slowness, but is patient toward you, not wishing that any should perish, but that all should reach repentance."

I have known of instances where family members of a terminal patient are not believers, but, where the one afflicted is a strong follower of the Lord. I have seen miracles happen to those loved ones through the devoted walk of one who is ill, but who throughout it all never loses faith. Often, the example set by a faithful follower can help bring others to saving Grace. To some of those left behind this might seem like a loss, because alas, their loved one has passed on. I look at instances such as these as a win. The afflicted one has crossed into glory. And for him/her to know that those left behind are covered by the blood of Jesus is a blessing unlike any other we can imagine.

Let's face it. We will all die, unless Jesus returns to collect His church before our earthly demise, so to be healed spiritually is the greatest healing of all. In this healing, this transition from spiritual death to spiritual life, you will gain eternal life with the Father. Yes, God still heals and yes, beloved, He still performs miracles every single day.

How About Tongues? Are They Real? Should We Speak in Tongues?

Speaking in tongues. This is one that causes much controversy. There are whole denominations that are so caught up with speaking in tongues that they will tell you if you have not yet spoken in tongues you are not saved. I don't recall anywhere in scripture that this was a prerequisite to being saved. As a matter of fact, in the book of Acts, the 16th chapter we read that at about midnight when Paul and Silas were praying and singing in their cell, suddenly the prison where they were being kept was shaken by an earthquake which opened all the doors and broke the bonds of every prisoner. The prison guard woke and became afraid that all the prisoners had escaped. He drew his sword and was about to kill himself. Paul shouted for him to stop, telling him that they were all still there. The jailer rushed in trembling in fear and fell before Paul and Silas. What happens next tells us all we need to know. Acts 16:30-31 "Then he brought them out and said, "Sirs, what must I do to be saved?" And they said, "Believe in the Lord Jesus, and you will be saved, you and your household."

Tongues is a subject my husband and I debated for years, before we did exhaustive study and found some true clarity on the subject. You see, he'd gone to churches which had gone to seed on tongues. I, on the other hand, had encountered some very negative experiences of walking into congregations who were all babbling incoherently in "other" tongues and I felt so out of place I simply snuck out and never returned.

We have discovered there is absolutely a place for tongues if used in the way for which they were designed. 1 Corinthians 14:1-33 is quite telling. It reads, "Pursue love, and earnestly desire the spiritual gifts, especially that you may prophesy. For one who speaks in a tongue speaks not to men but to God; for no one understands him, but he utters mysteries in the Spirit. On the other hand, the one who prophesies speaks to people for their up building, encouragement and consolation. The one who speaks in a tongue builds up himself, but the one who prophesies builds up the church. Now I want you all to speak in tongues, but even more to prophesy. The one who prophesies is greater than the one who speaks in tongues, unless someone interprets, so that the church may be built up.

"Now, brothers, if I come to you speaking in tongues, how will I benefit you unless I bring you some revelation or knowledge or prophecy or teaching? If even lifeless instruments, such as the flute or the harp, do not give distinct notes, how will anyone know what is played? And if the bugle gives an indistinct sound, who will get ready for the battle? So, with yourselves, if with your tongue you utter speech that is not intelligible, how will anyone know what is said? For you will be speaking into the air. There are doubtless many different languages in the world, and none is without meaning, but if I do not know the meaning of the language, I will be a foreigner to the speaker and the speaker a foreigner to me. So, with yourselves, since you are eager for manifestations of the Spirit, strive to excel in building up the church.

"Therefore, one who speaks in a tongue should pray for the power to interpret. For if I pray in a tongue, my spirit prays but my mind is unfruitful. What am I to do? I will pray with my spirit, but I will pray with my mind also. I will sing praise with my spirit, but I will sing with my mind also. Otherwise, if you give thanks with your spirit, how can anyone in the position of an outsider say "Amen" to your thanksgiving when he does not know what you are saying? For you may be giving thanks well enough, but the other person is not being built up. I thank God that I speak in tongues more than all of you. Nevertheless, in church I would rather speak five words with my mind in order to instruct others, than ten thousand words in a tongue.

"Brothers do not be children in your thinking. Be infants in evil, but in your thinking be mature. In the law it is written, "By people of strange tongues and by the lips of foreigners will I speak to this people, and even then, will they not listen to me, says the Lord" Thus tongues are a sign not for believers but for unbelievers, while prophecy is a sign not for unbelievers but for believers. If therefore the whole church comes together and all speak in tongues, and outsiders or unbelievers enter, will they not say that you are out of your minds? But if all prophesy, and an unbeliever or outsider enters, he is convicted by all, he is called to account by all, the secrets of his heart are disclosed, and so, falling on his face, he will worship God and declare that God is really among you."

To be clear, there is nothing wrong with speaking in tongues. I am not making light of tongues or making fun of tongues. However, Paul makes a distinction when he tells us that we should not be seeking tongues, but prophecy, in order to build up the church. If we go back to the original translation from Greek for 1 Corinthians and the Book of Acts, we see that two different words are used for tongues. Glossolalia, which is defined by linguists as fluid vocalizing of speech-like syllables that lack any readily comprehended meaning (or, in layman's terms, the "unknown" language); and xenolalia, which is defined as a natural, or known language, which is previously unknown to the speaker. In Acts 2 the followers of Jesus receive the Holy Spirit and speak in the languages of at least fifteen countries and ethnic groups. This is xenolalia.

When Paul is admonishing the Corinthian church, he is referring to the use of glossolalia in a public setting, particularly within the church. He tells us that we should not seek to speak in tongues, edifying only ourselves or trying to make ourselves look holy to others, but rather to do things which would build up the church such as using the gift of prophesy. You see, speaking in tongues, or glossolalia, is the easiest of all the gifts of the spirit to fake, and the people of the church in Corinth were doing a lot of that. Paul was telling us not to misuse the gifts.

Paul's advice is to keep the use of glossolalia mostly to our time with God, and within our personal prayer closet. He suggested that if we feel we must use this personal prayer language in church, to make sure we have an interpretation and even then, not to allow more than a couple of examples, so that people don't get caught up in that. Now, he never suggests that we should limit the use of xenolalia, as that language would be a gift which is a specific act of God. If there is a person who enters the congregation who speaks a natural language unknown to the speaker and God places this natural language, by the Holy Spirit, into the mouth and spirit of the speaker in order to share the Gospel, then this is a way to reach a non-believer with the message of Jesus Christ. That is a miracle of God and should never be questioned.

Tongues is a glorious way to communicate with the Father in your personal prayer closet. I highly suggest this form of communication. One of the differences between God and the Devil is that God knows your every thought and Satan does not. If you are communicating with the Lord in your personal prayer language God knows what you are saying. Even when you are distraught and don't know yourself what you should be praying. However, Satan does not understand that prayer language and does not read minds. Therefore, he does not know how to attack you in that matter. This is a powerful tool for the believer.

Don't be afraid of tongues. Your personal prayer language, or glossolalia, is simply whatever flows from your mouth when the spirit gives you utterance. It doesn't have to be anything fancy and the only ones who need to hear it are you and the Father. If you've never taken advantage of this gift, then the next time you are alone in prayer reach out to God with words only He will understand. Unburden your spirit.

Is Satan Real and Are There Actual Places Called Hell and Heaven?

This might seem an odd question, but it is one we hear frequently. Strangely it is not only non-believers who ask this one, but Christians who say that if God were good, as we believe He is, He wouldn't condemn anyone to hell, would He? This is a question I will answer later. You might think that if one has ever read the Bible, they would know the answer to this question, concerning the reality of Satan, Heaven and Hell already, but it seems there are many Christians who have never read the Bible and others who don't believe God's Word to be inerrant and infallible.

Since I am coming at all the questions in this book from a Biblical perspective, I will confess that I believe God's Word to be just that, God's Word, infallible and inerrant.

First, let's clear up the obvious. Who is Satan? The Hebrew word "Satan" means accuser or adversary. Satan is literally the accuser of the brethren (or, more precisely, Christians). Many believe he is currently bound in hell, but though he will be there in the future, I don't see Biblical evidence that hell is necessarily his present-day residence. In Revelation 20 verse 3, which most Biblical scholars perceive as events which will occur in the future we read, "Then I saw an angel coming down from heaven, holding in his hand the key to the bottomless pit and a great chain. And he seized the dragon, that ancient serpent, who is the devil and Satan, and bound him for a thousand years, and threw him into the pit and shut it and sealed it over him, so that he might not deceive the nations any longer, until the thousand years were ended. After that he must be released for a little while."

If we look around today; we can clearly see the influences of Satan surrounding us. So, for all intents and purposes, it doesn't appear he is currently bound in hell. Indeed, in 1 Peter 5:8 we read, "Be sober-minded; be watchful. Your adversary the devil prowls around like a roaring lion, seeking someone to devour." Satan is alive and well on planet earth and wreaking havoc everywhere he goes.

As for hell. Jesus talks more about hell than He talks about heaven and describes it more vividly. There is no doubt that He believes in and warns us about hell.

In Luke 16, Jesus describes a great chasm over which "none may cross from there to us." When reading Matthew 25 we see that Jesus tells of a time when people will be separated into two groups, one entering into His presence and the other banished to "eternal fire".

Jesus doesn't just reference hell, He describes it in detail: A place of eternal torment, Luke 16:23. A place of unquenchable fire, Mark 9:43. Where the worm does not die, Mark 9:48. A place where people will gnash their teeth in anguish and regret, Matthew 13:42. A place from which there is no return, even to warn your loved ones,

Luke 16:19-31. He calls hell a place of "outer darkness", Matthew 25:30. Comparing it to "Gehenna", Matthew 10:28, which was a garbage dump outside the walls of Jerusalem where trash was burned continually, and maggots abounded.

Ah, Heaven. A much more desirable subject and certainly a more recommended destination. Does Jesus mention Heaven? Let's see what the Word of God says.

Revelation 4:1-2 says, "After this I looked, and behold, a door standing open in Heaven! And the first voice, which I had heard speaking to me like a trumpet, said, "Come up here and I will show you what must take place after this. At once I was in the Spirit, and behold, a throne stood in Heaven, with one seated on the throne."

In Matthew 5:19 we read, "Therefore whoever

relaxes one of the least of these commandments and teaches others to do the same will be called least in the Kingdom of Heaven, but whoever does them and teaches them will be called great in the Kingdom of Heaven." And Matthew 5:12, "Rejoice and be glad, for your reward is great in heaven, for so they prosecuted the prophets who were before you." See also, 1 Corinthians 2:9; 2 Peter 3:13; 1 Corinthians 15:50; Revelation 21:1-5; Hebrews 11:16; and Revelation 22:1-5.

Obviously, when we read the words of Jesus, we see that He believed in literal places called Hell and Heaven. If we are looking from a Biblical perspective, we cannot deny that these places are real.

Why Would a Loving God Condemn People to Hell?

It's ironic that we get this question most from a certain group of people. This group of people have usually come to us because they are involved in something that they are ashamed of or are feeling guilty about and they're afraid they are headed to that dreadful place. I would like to say first that it is not my job to judge, but when I share scripture it is also not my job to nullify the Word of God (as if I would ever have that kind of power) simply because it does not suit someone's feelings or agenda.

We talk to people all the time, who when

asked if they will be going to Heaven, inevitably say, "Of course I'm going to Heaven. I'm a good person" or, "Why wouldn't I go to Heaven? I've never..........". We continue to share the Gospel with those people and with anyone who does not turn away.

The reason Jesus talked so much about hell is because it is the fate that awaits every single person who is spiritually apart from Him. Because of Adam's sin, we are all guilty (whether you think that sounds fair or not), and we all deserve God's eternal punishment. Contrary to popular belief, hell is not a place where God sends those who have been especially bad. Hell is our default destination. If we do not make a choice for Jesus, then we make a choice against Jesus. It's simple. We need a rescuer, or we stand condemned.

We are left with two options: stay in a place of depravity, away from the Lord, or submit to the Savior and accept His gift of redemption.

The single truth that allows me to accept the justice of hell is the certainty of the absolute goodness of God. While the concept of hell is difficult to grasp, Jesus, with His nail scarred hands is worthy of my everlasting trust. His goodness causes me to draw closer to Him, looking ultimately to the cross.

God's greatness causes me to bow my knee, cry out in wonder and fear Him. I know I don't "deserve" salvation. I deserve punishment. However, His goodness causes me to rise in endless praise, grateful for a Savior who was willing to die for me.

His goodness allows me, and you, to enter

His presence boldly and without fear. Because He alone is good, I can have a relationship with Him as a beloved child, snatched from the flames of hell.

Who Created God?

This is a good one and it always makes me smile. We talk to people all the time who ask this question. You know, I have to say that if God was a created being, He simply wouldn't be God in my humble estimation.

The Bible is very consistent in this matter. The view regarding God is that He did not come from anywhere. He is the creator of the universe and no one "made" the creator of the universe. He had no beginning, and He will have no end. He is the eternal, self-existing Being. Here is what the Bible says about the existence of God:

God is eternal

Isaiah 40:28 "Have you not known? Have you not heard? The Lord is the everlasting God, the creator of the ends of the earth. He does not faint or grow weary; His understanding is unsearchable.

Romans 16:26 "but has now been disclosed and through the prophetic writings has been made known to all nations, according to the command of the eternal God, to bring about the obedience of faith.

1 Timothy 1:17 "To the King of ages, immortal, invisible, the only God, be honor and glory forever and ever. Amen."

Psalm 90:2 "Before the mountains were brought forth, or ever you had formed the earth and the world, from everlasting to everlasting you are God."

God is self-existing

The Lord revealed Himself to Moses as the "I AM THAT I AM" in Exodus 3:13-17 "Then Moses said to God, "If I come to the people of Israel and say to them, "The God of your fathers has sent me to you" and they ask me, "What is His Name?" what shall I say to them? God said to Moses, "I AM WHO I AM." God also said to Moses, "Say this to the people of Israel, "The Lord, the God of your fathers, the God of Abraham, the God of Isaac, and the God of Jacob, has sent me to you. This is my Name forever, and thus I am to be remembered throughout all generations."

The "I AM" expression is related to the Hebrew

Name for God, "Yahweh" (Lord, or Jehovah). This was the most sacred Name for God.

The term Yahweh occurs more than 6,800 times in the Old Testament. The word is believed to be a form of the verb "hayah", which signifies "to be," ultimately meaning "the eternal One" or "self-existing One."

God's existence is underived; no one made Him. He simply always was.

Now let's look at a God who has always existed from a scientific, logical perspective, because many people will refuse to believe what is right in front of them without scientific evidence. So, here we go.

Logically speaking the universe must have been created by something. If there ever was a time when "nothing" at all existed, then there would be absolutely nothing today.

It is an axiomatic truth that if nothing exists, then "nothing" will be the case – always, for nothing simply remains nothing – forever! Nothing plus nothing equals nothing.

If there is absolutely nothing but nothing, there cannot ever be something. "Nothing" and "something"—applied to the same object, at the same time—are mutually exclusive terms. Hence, something has always existed. Since it is the case that something now exists, one must logically conclude that something has always existed.

Let us state the matter again: If nothing cannot produce something, and yet something exists, then it follows necessarily that something has always existed.

Now we must ask ourselves: What is the

"something" that has always existed?

Is the "something" an eternal non-material spirit being?

In the study of logic there is a law. That law is called the "law of the excluded middle". The law states that a thing either is, or it is not. A line is either straight, or it is not straight. Pretty straight forward, huh?

Now, let's apply this law to the subject at hand. Something has existed forever. That "something" must be either material in nature or non-material.

If it can be shown that the eternal "something" is not material in nature, then it logically follows that the eternal "something" is non-material in nature. Another term for "non-material" would be "spirit."

So, let us use common sense. The question now becomes, what does the available evidence reveal? Has "matter" existed forever, or does the evidence argue instead that the eternal "something" is non-matter? And since we have already established that non-matter is spirit, then we now must consider a spiritual being.

The most reputable scientists in the world concede that matter is not eternal. In his book, "Until the Sun Dies", Dr. Robert Jastrow, founder of NASA's Goddard Institute for Space Studies and a professed agnostic, described his perception of the initial creation of the universe.

He spoke of that moment when "the first particles of matter appear", thus, prior to that moment in his knowledgeable estimation, matter did not exist. Subsequently, he declared emphatically that "modern science denies an eternal existence to the universe?".

There is not a speck of evidence that the universe has existed forever. The very fact that scientists make one attempt after another to assign an "age" to the universe is revealing within itself, because any age at all would tell us that there was a time before that age, no matter how long ago it was, when there was 'nothing'.

Okay then, in view of this information, namely that something has always existed and yet that "something" is not of a material nature, the student of logic is forced to the obvious conclusion that the "something" that is eternal is non-material and that this non-material eternal something must be spirit in its essence.

In John 4:24 we are told that God is an

uncreated eternal Spirit Being, so, we have shown both in Scripture and through logic that God has always existed. He is the everlasting I AM. No one made Him. He simply IS.

Is God an Uncaring Egomaniac?

Someone asked me this question a few months ago. Her reasoning, she said, was that several terrible things had happened in her family over the past year and she didn't see evidence that God had been there for her at all.

She declared there were times, when she was sitting on her porch swing in the cool of the evening, when she imagined God lounging on His throne in Heaven looking down on her and laughing at her troubles.

She wondered why He bothered to make mankind at all if He was just going to leave us floundering around down here on our own. Or perhaps, she added, He simply derived some sort of perverse pleasure from watching us fall on our faces time and again.

My heart broke for her, but at the same time I knew she was very mistaken. Of course, God cares about us. He certainly wouldn't have come to die for us in the most heinous and painful way if He didn't care. Would you ever have done the same? I'm darned sure I wouldn't have.

He surely wouldn't have left His throne in heaven to dwell with us, so that we might know Him in a personal way, if He gained pleasure in our troubles. He died and rose again to overcome death for our sakes. He was already living in paradise. He created the earth and all its beauty for us, His children.

Having said that, we do live in a fallen world.

A fallen world, because of man's sin not God's sin. In a fallen world there is trouble and strife. However, if you have a relationship with Jesus; if you've made Him the Lord of your life, then you have an advocate. You can go to God in prayer. You can trust in Him to walk beside you in all of life's trials. Prayer works. Believe in Him.

Is God uncaring? I don't know about you, but I'm a terrible person as far as people go. I've done lots of things in this life that I'm not proud of and left undone many that I should have taken care to finish. Is God uncaring? In my book anyone who would leave the joys of heaven to come and save me, a terrible person, is more amazing than words can say. Romans 5:6-7 says it best, "For while we were still weak, at the right time Christ died for the ungodly. For one will scarcely die for a righteous person – though perhaps for a good person one would dare even to die – but God shows His love for us in that while we were still sinners, Christ died for us."

Though I'd like to think I've come a long way in Christ since first we met, I also know there is much yet to be accomplished in my character. God is still working on me, so praise be to Him there is hope yet to make this imperfect person a godly representative of Jesus on the earth.

Is God an egomaniac? Since the definition of "egomaniac" is excessive self-centeredness I have a hard time believing this. Did you know that there are more than 17,500 varieties of butterfly in the world and over 391,000 kinds of plants and flowers? Would a self-centered God create so much variety for our pleasure and enjoyment when He could easily have gotten away with perhaps a dozen or so and we would never have known the difference? I think not. God didn't just make us a place to live during our time here on this earthly plain, He created for us a place of great beauty. Would a self-centered Being do that?

Now, having said that, God is a jealous God. He has made Himself available to us through Jesus' sacrifice on the cross. He wants relationship with His children, and He has made it clear that, though He loves us all enough to die for us, this relationship is available only to those who believe that Jesus is God's Son and that He died and rose again for their individual sins. If your idea of enlarged ego is a God who expects His followers to confess their sin and to

Invite Him into their hearts, in order to know eternity with Him in heaven, then I suppose that is your opinion. However, if you have not already done so. He is waiting with open arms.

How Can You Possibly Believe in a 6 Day Creation Scenario? What About Evolution?

Here we go again. These are questions we get on an ongoing basis and not just from non-Christians. I don't know if you can imagine how many people who call themselves Christians come up with different variations of these questions.

Because I am a believer in the inerrant, infallible Word of God, but also a lover of science, I will be answering these questions from both perspectives.

First, I must admit that I get tired of hearing

people claim that evolution is a proven scientific fact. **Scientific facts** are verified by repeatable careful observation or measurement by experiments or other means. Since both 'creation' and 'evolution' would have transpired before mankind existed in a state to do any of these things, neither theory can be verified, repeated, or observed by experiments or any other means, so they are both simply theories. This is where faith comes in. In what do you base your faith, the Word of God, or the word of man? Well, here are some thoughts, insights, and scriptures to help you decide.

Let's first define "Day" from the Hebrew text. This will give us a better concept of that troublesome word and get the whole "Literal 6 Days" figured out. The word 'Yom', in the Hebrew text of Genesis 1, ALWAYS means an ordinary day when used with a modifying number (1, 2, 3, 1st, 2nd, 3rd, etc.) This is its meaning in all other 358 times it is used outside of the Genesis 1 text, so why would Genesis 1 be an exception?

As a defining phrase, "evening and morning" is mentioned a total of 38 times outside of that Genesis 1 text and in every one of those cases it ALWAYS means an ordinary day. Again, why would Genesis 1 be any different?

Yom is never used to mean a long period of time, such as the geological ages.

Yamin (plural, "days") is used 700+ times in the Old Testament, and in every case, it refers clearly to a regular day.

God Himself distinguishes days from years in Genesis 1:14.

In Exodus 20:11 we are told that God worked for 6 days and rested for 1 day to give us a pattern to follow in our own daily lives. Therefore, making 1 day = thousands, millions or billions of years makes no logical sense.

Some have tried to take scriptures like Psalm 90:4 and 2 Peter 3:8, where the authors are telling us that to God a day is like a thousand years and a thousand years like a day, completely out of context. This is very confusing for those who want to know but have not studied the text thoroughly. The Psalm in question is referring to the fact that time is not relevant to God, because He exists outside of time; and the verse in 2 Peter is commenting on the scoffers who will come to laugh at those of us who are waiting for Christ's return, suggesting that His coming will happen quickly and that they should prepare before they are lost, because God doesn't want anyone to be lost.

Why does it matter how others interpret God's Word, and whether we believe them or not? Because we should never allow the fallible theories of mere men to dictate to us what the words in the Bible mean. We should take God at His Word. When it is this obvious from the words and their context what the meaning is, then accept this and stop trying to make God's Word mean something other than what He intended it to mean.

I hear too many people use the "most of the Bible cannot be taken literally" comment, way too often. Yes, there are some examples such as in Revelation and some of the various prophet's writings about future events, where those future events are not completely understood by the writer. But that is because those future events were being seen in the spirit by someone from the past who did not recognize many of the objects and scenarios, he was able see in those visions. However, most of the Bible is very clear and understandable. Stop allowing another's doubt to creep into your own thought process.

Some would have you doubt 6 days simply because if they can give you cause to doubt one part of the Word, then it is easier to make you doubt other parts of the Word. The only way to keep this from happening is to study. Get into the Word. Read the scriptures and study to show yourself approved as Paul tells us to do in 2 Timothy 2:15.

Look around. God's creation and His science is all around you. He is the only one in the universe who can lay claim to that 'science' after all, because He was the only one there to observe its inception as He created it all.

I have been asked how the morning and the evening were considered the first day when the stars, sun and moon had not yet been created. Where was the light? The day/night cycle is evidence of a regular rotation of the earth, which does not contradict science, but is mutually supported by scientific observation. If you read Revelation 22:5 you will see that the Lord God will be our light in the new city of Jerusalem, which comes down from heaven to be our new home. That being the case and God being the source of all light, God simply was the light in the beginning, and He will be our light in the new city.

In exodus 20:11 we read: "For in six days the Lord made the heavens and the earth, the sea, and all that is in them, and rested the seventh day. Therefore, the Lord blessed the Sabbath day and hallowed it." This, of course, is the basis of our seven-day week – six days of work and one day of rest. Obviously, this passage was meant to be taken as speaking of a total of seven literal days based on the Creation Week of six literal days of work and one literal day of rest.

Now, I believe we have established to some degree of certainty that the Bible's interpretation of a day is a literal day, and that God is specific about His creation taking 6 literal days. So, let's move on to the controversial topic of, Theories of Origins.

There are four prevailing theories regarding the origin of the universe, the earth and life itself predominant in our culture – both secular and Judeo/Christian. Here is a short description of each one:

1. Naturalism (Naturalistic Evolution)- Naturalism allows no room for God, including miracles or divine intervention. This theory posits that natural processes can explain everything. Evolution is based on naturalism.

2. Theistic Evolution - This theory claims that God created matter and then everything else evolved with or without occasional help from God. Some will even go as far as saying God directed the evolutionary

process. It's basically evolution with God added as an afterthought to keep the Creationists happy. This position denies the truth of Scripture.

3. Old Earth Creation or Progressive Creation- In this theory the "days" of creation are long periods of time or ages (usually millions or billions of years) during which God created the universe and all its contents. The plan is to make evolution and the geologic column basically fit with the sequence of events of the creation week, although you must really twist and creatively interpret the text to make it do so. Unfortunately, many Christians have bought into this theory because it sounds somewhat plausible. However, in Mark

10:6, Jesus combined Genesis 1 creation days with creation of man as happening at the same time, not millions of years later, so someone has miscalculated. I don't think it was Jesus. Even evolutionists question why any Christian worth his salt would believe this position.

4. Young Earth Creation or Literal Creation- Young earth creationists adhere to the plain reading of Biblical text. This position believes that God did His creating just as He told us He did in Genesis 1 and 2. This position is easiest to describe and explain but the hardest for many to accept even when it is plainly understood, due usually to a lack of faith in the infallibility of the Word of God.

My personal scientific belief in a creation theory is based largely on the two most fundamental laws in the entire science realm, the first and second laws of thermodynamics. These laws are the basic common sense of sound science. The first law states that energy is always conserved or constant. Energy, in whichever of its many forms indicated, cannot be created or destroyed. This rule ensures a predictable and dependable universe, whether for stars or for humans.

Energy conservation was likely established at the completion of creation week. At this time the Creator ceased the input of energy into the physical universe from His infinite reserves. This fundamental law of energy simply cannot be disobeyed like a man-made law. Only our

Creator God has the power to lay aside His laws, for example, with a miracle.

The second basic law of thermodynamics (entropy) also involves energy. Unavoidable losses in any process in which the transfer of energy is involved. The energy does not disappear. However, some always becomes unavailable, often as unusable heat. If we state this in another way, everything breaks down or deteriorates and becomes less ordered with time (throwing a wrench in the idea of evolution which demands that things become more ordered with time in order to 'evolve'). Ultimately, even death is a consequence of the second law of thermodynamics. This rule is related to the Curse placed upon nature at the fall of mankind in Eden.

Energy conservation tells us that the universe didn't start up all by itself. Energy decay implies that this universe can't last forever. Evolution cannot explain how an organism could go through millions or billions of years of development, when in fact it has begun to decay from the very moment of physical inception.

Secular science simply has no satisfactory explanation for such laws of nature. The purveyors of the theory of evolution simply hope that their followers will not seek out the science and make conclusions based on common sense. These rules and principles transcend natural science. Their origin is supernatural, which does not require long ages to develop. These laws are entirely consistent with the biblical, six-day creation.

Jesus clearly taught that the creation was

young, for when He spoke Adam and Eve existed "from the beginning," (found in Mark 10:6) not millions or billions of years after the universe and the earth came into existence.

In human genetics, the **Mitochondrial Eve** is the matrilineal most recent common ancestor (MRCA) of all living humans. In other words, she is defined as the most recent woman from whom all living humans descend in an unbroken line purely through their mothers and through the mothers of those mothers, back until all lines converge on one woman. Yes, we are truly all family.

Colossians makes it clear that Jesus, the Son of God, was the one who created all things: "For by Him all things were created that are in heaven and that are on earth, visible and invisible, whether thrones or dominions or principalities or powers. All things were created through Him and for Him. And He is before all things, and in Him all things consist." Colossians 1:16-17.

We also know that Jesus is called the Word: "In the beginning was the Word, and the Word was with God, and the Word was God. He was in the beginning with God. All things were made through Him, and without Him nothing was made that was made." John 1:1-3.

As human beings living in an imperfect, sinful world, sometimes our eyes don't give us an accurate view of what we see around us. Our vision can be clouded by many things – preconceived ideas, fear, sinful attitudes, or the enemy. Emotions are changeable and often deceptive, which distorts our perception. What this worldly culture presents as truth has often been twisted and molded to fit a particular bias or agenda.

When Jesus referred to God's Word, He didn't use an adjective; He didn't say it was "true." He used a noun, "truth," implying that the Word is the only standard of truth against which everything else must be evaluated. John 17:17 "Sanctify them in the truth, Your Word is truth." And Psalm 119:160, "The sum of Your Word is truth, and every one of Your righteous rules endures forever."

Jesus, who is the Word, created everything by simply speaking things into existence and that is truth.

Do You Believe We Are Facing an Impending Climate Catastrophe? What is Our Duty, as Christians, to the Earth God has Given Us for a Habitation?

Ice Age, Global Warming and Climate Change. All controversial terms.

This can be a very touchy subject for some, as the merest suggestion that "Climate Change" isn't everything it's cracked up to be gains an attack from those who will accuse us of not caring about the earth.

I remember very clearly in their June 24, 1974 issue, when Time magazine presented an article entitled "Another Ice Age?" The article noted that the atmosphere had been growing gradually cooler for the past three decades. The panic began.

For those of you who might remember that time, this was a very serious topic and garnered worldwide attention. New construction house sizes became smaller by half due to concern over how they would be heated in the coming "Ice Age". Gasoline prices soared over thoughts of shortages, with the idea of upcoming winters. There was talk of our planet eventually becoming a ball of ice floating in space. I remember it well.

I must admit that since I was much younger

then and had not lived through as much manufactured hysteria as I have now witnessed, I too was sucked into the hype. I have since learned that those who sell the panic also sell the pill and become very wealthy doing so. Now I tend to seek out the science and what the Word of God says, before I decide on what course to take, or who to believe. I find that far too many do not do so.

There is a tendency by much of the world, especially those who do not have a strong relationship with the Lord, to feed into the hype and hysteria of every so-called crisis. I also know that part of the Marxist playbook, according to Saul Alinsky, is to never let a good crisis go to waste, but to use it to their advantage and for their gain toward that ever-present goal of socialism and a one world government. I don't find that to be helpful to those who are seeking solutions to the problems.

Soon, after the 1974 pronouncement that the world would be enveloped in ice, a young Al Gore, at the age of twenty-eight joined the United States House of Representatives. In 1976 he held the first congressional hearings on toxic waste and "global warming". He continued to speak on this topic all through the 1980s, becoming quite wealthy in the process.

In February 2007, the day after his extremely panic inducing film "An Inconvenient Truth" won an Academy Award for best documentary (making him all the wealthier), a shocking public record backed report revealed Al Gore's Nashville home used twenty times more electricity than that of the average American household.

After backlash for his electricity use, the former vice president pledged to renovate his house to make it more energy efficient. The expensive overhaul of his house included solar panels and geothermal heating.

Years after those renovations, the National Center for Public Policy Research obtained the electricity usage information of the Gore household through public records and requests to the Nashville Electric Service. Those records showed that in 2016 Gore's home energy use averaged 19,241 Kilowatt hours every month, compared to the U.S. household average of 901 kWh per month. Telling us that Al Gore, the "self-appointed spokesman" of the environmental movement uses more electricity in one year than the average American family uses in twenty-one years. Obviously, he was not nearly as concerned about the demise of civilization, through global warming. as he has led us to believe.

The terminology has now evolved into "Climate Change", from Ice Age and Global Warming, but it is still accomplishing the same degree of panic and lining the pockets of some very influential people. I often wonder why so many celebrities and politicians' shouting the loudest about "Climate Change" are the one's circling the globe in private jets and leaving "Big Foot sized" carbon footprints. That fact alone ought to give us all pause concerning their true intentions and motives.

Now, having said all that, I know from Scripture that the earth is God's. We have been given a gift and the responsibility to care for this amazing gift. Psalm 24:1-2, "The earth is the Lord's and the fullness thereof, the world and those who dwell therein, for He has founded it upon the seas and established it upon the rivers." Genesis 2:15, "The Lord God took the man and put him in the garden of Eden to work it and keep it." And Proverbs 12:10, "Whoever is righteous has regard for the life of his beast, but the mercy of the wicked is cruel."

However, when I hear many "earthers" declare that plants and animals are more valuable than mankind, that we simply evolved from the muck and are of no more worth than a worm, or that the earth would be better off without humans, I must disagree. God created us in His image and considers us valuable enough to die for. He does not offer the same gift of eternal life to the beasts of the field. To claim anything different is simply not true. Genesis 1:26-31, "Then God said, "Let us make man in our image, after Our likeness. And let them have dominion over the fish of the sea and over the birds of the heavens and over the livestock and over all the earth and over every creeping thing that creeps on the earth." So, God created man in His own image, in the image of God He created him; male and female He created them. And God blessed them. And God said to them, "Be fruitful and multiply and fill the earth and subdue it and have dominion over the fish of the sea and over the birds of the heavens and over every living thing that moves on the earth." And God said, "Behold, I have given you every plant yielding seed that is on the face of all the earth, and every tree with seed in its fruit. You shall have them for food. And to every beast of the earth and to every bird of the heavens and to everything that creeps on the earth, everything that has the breath of life, I have given every green plant for food." And it was so. And God saw everything that He had made, and behold, it was very good. And there was evening and there was morning, the sixth day."

Does this mean I don't see the things going on around us that do damage to the earth and our environment? Of course not. Or that I don't recognize the horrible cruelty inflicted on some of God's creatures by many? I should say not. These things need to be addressed in the strongest of terms. However, to claim that mankind has no place on the earth God created for our habitation is ludicrous.

As with all things, it is interesting to explore what the Bible says about the importance of caring for the earth and its environment.

The late evangelist, Billy Graham once said that, "Of all people, Christians should be the most concerned for the environment," explaining that God created the world and entrusted humanity to protect it. "When we see the world as a gift from God, we will do our best to take care of it and use it wisely, instead of poisoning or destroying it."

Sadly, this is not always the case. We must cherish our dwelling place and leave the earth as an inheritance for our children and grandchildren.

Does God Get Mad When We are Angry With Him, Or When We Doubt Him?

Our Heavenly Father is a loving God. Remember, He is all-knowing. When we're upset with Him, He already knows. Heck, He even understands our reasons for being angry better than we do. However, it is still important for us to communicate what He already knows with Him. It helps to keep our own minds and hearts invested in the relationship we have with Him and it helps us to hear Him speak to our hearts. This will eventually resolve our feelings toward Him and give us peace as we maintain open lines. The worst thing we can do is to cut off communication with the only One who has the true power and desire to help us through our troubles.

I have some Bible verses to share. Verses you can pray, which will help when you are feeling angry with God, or when you feel that He has forgotten or abandoned you.

"Well, goodie," you might be thinking (perhaps sarcastically). "I've been doing that already and that's why I'm mad at Him. He isn't answering me. So, He's either forgotten all about me, or He just doesn't care."

I have news for you. You aren't the first person to feel this way. Did you know that the Bible is chock full of people who've had experiences like yours? I have also felt that way in the past.

I used to think that if I prayed about something my prayers should be answered right now and in exactly the way I had decided beforehand that they should be answered.

I have since discovered that I serve a God who is much wiser and more informed than I am on all subjects concerning my life, my health, my mental well-being and my future. I used to wonder why bad things happened and feel that though I certainly deserved all the evil things that came my way, He didn't need to keep rubbing my nose in the fact that I was less than desirable and totally not worthy to be loved.

Then, I started to notice that when I let go and let God take over; when I trusted Him for the best; when I believed in His promises from scripture, all things began to turn around for my good. Though He didn't hold it against me when I'd felt unloved and forgotten, or when I was madder than heck at Him, He proved to me over and over that His intentions toward me were for good and not for evil.

Romans 8:28 tells us, "And we know that for those who love God all things work together for good, for those who are called according to His purpose." And in Genesis 50:20 we read, "As for you, you meant evil against me, but God meant it for good, to bring it about that many people should be kept alive, as they are today."

I assure you that God loves you. Even if you have never asked Jesus into your heart, God loves you. He came to earth as a man named Jesus and died for you, to give you the opportunity to be saved and spend eternity with Him. It is your choice to accept that gift of Jesus' sacrifice on the cross for your redemption.

if you have already decided to live for Christ, you have an advocate with the Father. One you can trust to be ever mindful of what is best for you at every turn. He knows your past and your future. He can determine how things will work out, so if something seems amiss at this moment, it may be the very thing that is needed to get you to where you need to be.

I have a friend who broke her leg recently. It was a bad break, and she was angry with God that it should happen when the holidays are drawing near. After all, He should know how busy her schedule was, shouldn't He? On top of that she watches her tiny, new granddaughter several days a week, and wouldn't be able to do that with surgery coming up. Before the surgery to repair the complicated break, an MRI was done that revealed other issues. After further testing it was revealed that she had a rare cancer in the bone of her leg, which had gone entirely undetected.

Without the break, the cancer would not have been discovered until the situation was well past the point of no return. So that which seemed a tragedy at first, was a blessing in disguise. We didn't know, but God knew, and He used it for her good. This incident has brought her daughter home. A daughter who had been estranged from her for a decade. A daughter who had lost faith, but is now a believer again, due to this unpredictable miracle. By the way, the treatments are working wonderfully. And though she might not be as active this holiday season as she has been in the past, she is home with her family and alive. What a blessing.

After dealing with a ten-year cancer battle of my own, (which, praise God, is in complete remission now), and eleven surgeries throughout that ten years, I have concluded that the Father has everything under control. Each time something has come up, which seems a tragic event in that moment, more things are put right, and I grow in my understanding of His mighty omnipotence and Grace. More than once I have wondered what I was supposed to learn or gain from an ongoing experience, only to discover some wondrous new knowledge or even see a new soul come to know the Lord through my own experiences and my continued writing.

I am thoroughly convinced that we, as mere

humans, cannot comprehend fully the mind of God, and that if we just turn our lives over to Him and trust Him for the patience and grace to endure till the end, all will be well.

Now, when I learn of some new obstacle that the world, or indeed Satan, has placed in my path, I turn to God and pray, knowing that He has my back and the nature of my soon coming blessing will be made known to me in due time.

As I said before, there are many examples in scripture that show us how the prophets and psalmists have felt when dealing with those same feelings of abandonment and anger toward God. Here are a few examples:

Psalm 13:1-2 "How long, O Lord? Will You forget me forever? How long will you hide Your face from me?"

Habakkuk 1:2-4 "O Lord, how long shall I cry for help, and You will not hear? Or cry to You "Violence!" and You will not save? Why do You make me see iniquity, and why do You idly look at wrong? Destruction and violence are before me; strife and contention arise. So, the law is paralyzed, and justice never goes forth. For the wicked surround the righteous, so justice goes forth perverted."

Psalm 6:1-3 "O Lord, rebuke me not in Your anger, not discipline me in Your wrath. Be gracious to me, O Lord, for I am languishing; heal me, O Lord, for my bones are troubled. My soul also is greatly troubled. But You, O Lord – how long?"

Psalm 10:1 "Why, O Lord, do you stand far away? Why do You hide Yourself in times of trouble?"

Psalm 79:5 "How long, O Lord? Will You be angry forever? Will Your jealousy burn like fire?"

Psalm 89:46 "How long, O Lord? Will You hide Yourself forever? How long will Your wrath burn like fire?"

Lamentations 5:20 "Why do you forget us forever; why do you forsake us for so many days?"

Psalm 22:1 "My God, my God, why have You forsaken me? Why are You so far from saving me, from the words of my groaning?"

Psalm 42:9-10 "I say to God, my rock: "Why have You forgotten me? Why do I go mourning because of the oppression of the enemy? As with a deadly wound in my bones, my adversaries taunt me, while they say to me all the day long, "Where is your God?"

Jeremiah 12:1 "Righteous are You, O Lord, when I complain to You; yet I would plead my case before You. Why does the way of the wicked prosper? Why do all who are treacherous thrive?"

God wants us to give Him our hearts in whatever state they may be. It really doesn't make you a terrible person to be angry with Him. He is a big God, and He can handle your anger. He wants to heal you, to remedy your hurts. And He will, even if it takes some time. Just be honest with Him.

Remember though that we can't fake prayer, trying to fool God by simply going through the motions, or that relationship will suffer. Pulling ourselves away from Him doesn't make Him stop caring about us. He will always be "right here". However, if there is distance between us and

God, it is not He who has moved.

Okay, so God understands when we become angry with Him, but how does He feel about doubt?

Doubt is a completely different matter. It isn't a mere sense of anger at God for things that might be going wrong with our own self-defined life plan. Let's face it, anger at God ultimately proves that we believe He not only exists, but that He also has power over the outcome of things pertaining to our lives. Doubt, on the other hand, is unbelief, plain and simple. When we doubt, we are saying that perhaps there is no God, no power, no Jesus, no payment made for sin, no divine plan. God did not send His Son to die, to make a way of salvation for us, without great personal sacrifice. Hence, if we believe, we are saved; but if we do not believe, we are lost.

I lived with doubt for many years of my life. I doubted that any god could truly love me. I had been badly abused as a child and young woman and grew up to be a scarred, damaged, frightened and world hardened woman. I knew I'd done many things in my life to be ashamed of, during my years of rebellion and anger. I was positive I didn't deserve forgiveness. I was "dirty" after all.

What I didn't realize at that time was that it was not God who'd labeled me that way, but I. I spent years trying to prove to the world and to myself that I didn't need anyone, not even God. That I could do it all myself. I faked my way through life for many decades. However, as time went on, I was failing miserably. After my 2010 cancer diagnosis, which led to some serious soul searching and subsequent intense Bible study I realized how wrong I'd been, and I opened my heart to Jesus in a way I never had before. He freed me from years of doubt and rage to follow Him with joy.

John 3:18, "Whoever believes in Him is not condemned, but whoever does not believe is condemned already, because he has not believed in the Name of the only Son of God."

Doubt is a dangerous thing for a Christian and is always a threat to the relationship if we do not make a habit of talking with the Father daily. Doubt is an absence of faith. Doubt shuts God out and makes an easy path for Satan from which to attack. Here are a few more scriptures dealing with doubt.

James 1:5-8, "If any of you lacks wisdom, let him ask God, who gives generously to all without reproach, and it will be given him. But let him ask in faith, with no doubting, for the one who doubts is like a wave of the sea that is driven and tossed by the wind. For that person must not suppose that he will receive anything from the Lord; he is a double minded man, unstable in all his ways."

Matthew 21:21, Shows Jesus saying, "Truly I say to you, if you have faith and do not doubt, you will not only do what has been done to the fig tree, but even if you say to this mountain, 'be taken up and thrown into the sea,' it will happen"

Matthew 14:31, "Jesus immediately reached out His hand and took hold of him, saying to him, "O you of little faith, why did you doubt?"

Mark 9:24, "Immediately the father of the child cried out and said, "I believe; help my unbelief!"

John 20:24-29, "Now Thomas, one of the Twelve, called the Twin, was not with them when Jesus came. So, the other disciples told him, "We have seen the Lord." But he said to them, "Unless I see in His hands the mark of the nails and place my finger into the mark of the nails, and place my hand into His side, I will never believe." Eight days later, His disciples were inside again, and Thomas was with them. Although the doors were locked, Jesus came and stood among them and said, "Peace be with you." Then He said to Thomas, "Put your finger here and see my hands; and put out your hand and place it in my side. Do not disbelieve but believe." Thomas answered Him, "My Lord and my God!" Jesus said to Him, "Have you believed because you have seen me? Blessed are those who have not seen and yet have believed."

Hebrews 11:6, "And without faith it is impossible to please Him, for whoever would draw near to God must believe that He exists and that He rewards those who seek Him."

2 Corinthians 5:7, "For we walk by faith, not by sight."

Matthew 28:17, "And when they saw Him, they worshipped Him, but some doubted."

Romans 10:17, "So faith comes from hearing, and hearing through the Word of Christ."

Doubt, (lack of faith), is a serious barrier for Christians. Doubt creeps in when we don't know the Father's plans for us. But really, how can we know the Father's plans for us? Those plans are made abundantly clear in His Word. Keep up an ongoing conversation with your Heavenly Father. Go to a Bible believing church where you will find fellowship with like believers. Search out a like-minded study partner or mentor. Get into the Word and dig out the answers. Additionally, there are some great study Bibles available and many online sources, if you are truly interested. All you must really possess, if you are serious, is an earnest desire to learn more of Him and He will make a way.

God longs for communication with His beloved children. The amount of time you invest (through Bible study and prayer) in an intimate personal relationship with Him, will be the final determiner of your own degree of active faith or doubt. No fancy, made for television, prayers are necessary. Just talk to Him as you would a best friend and listen for the still small voice in your soul that will give you guidance, reassurance, and the love you so richly desire.

Should Christians be Involved in Politics?

A friend asked me this question the other day and I was surprised. It seems to come up exclusively during times of election, especially contentious ones, but I hadn't thought about it in a while. I guess I've always tended to have and express political opinions. I did a little checking and discovered what I consider to be a frightening fact. Around six in ten Christians believe that we should have no part in the politics of our nation. This is a shocking situation, because if we are not involved in the political workings of our country and simply leave it all to those who are not believers, what do you suppose the outcome of that strategy will be?

Well, here we are. Living in a nation that largely thinks abortion up to the moment of birth and in some cases, after birth, is perfectly fine. That the stripping away of our religious freedom, our right to free speech, our right to own and bear arms, along with many other freedoms, is no big deal. How many genders do we have currently? I've lost count. How do we impress our world view on the fabric of our nation? We must be involved, and it starts with voting.

But how do I vote? Simply, you view the platforms of those running for a particular office and choose the one whose beliefs and voting record most closely matches your own Christian values, no matter whether you like their personality, their tweets and their tone or not. Selecting our leaders should be less about a popularity contest and more about the welfare of our nation. To do otherwise will mean that someone with moral standards different than your own will inhabit that political space. If you don't think that makes a difference, look around you.

When Jesus walked on earth he didn't live in a democratic republic. The United States of America didn't exist at that time. Instead, He lived under an imperial dictatorship. He, along with the balance of the population, had no chance to cast a ballot. He declared: "Render to Caesar that which is Caesar's, and to God, the things that are God's."

Here we are in the twenty-first century. Instead of suggesting distance between believers and civil government, Jesus indicated there was a level of responsibility to get involved in civic matters. We have the God-given opportunity to select our own leaders, instead of having those leaders imposed upon us.

Let me ask you a question. Shouldn't God's people have a hand in matters that will influence the selection of our leaders and therefore our future and that of our children and grandchildren? A set of values will govern our nation. Will those moral values emulate that of the radical Left, the radical Right, or of those who follow the Almighty? Given what Scripture tells us about the character and nature of God, what do you think His thoughts would be on our leaders passing laws which promote the killing of our innocent unborn, or the destruction of the biblical definition of marriage? It only makes sense that Christians should be on the front lines of upholding His principles.

Some well-intentioned believers feel that any effort to shape the behavior of non-Christians is wrong.

Founding Father, John Jay, our first chief justice of the Supreme Court stated: "Providence has given to our people the choice of their rulers, and it is the duty, as well as the privilege and interest of our Christian nation to select and prefer Christians for their rulers."

Can you imagine any of our politicians saying that today? Well, at least not without the "Political Correctness" police immediately pouncing on them to censor them and shut them up.

In commanding His followers to be "salt" and "light" in the world, Jesus encourages us to influence our culture rather than isolating ourselves from it. I hear statements such as, "I personally believe in this, but I don't feel that I can impose my morality on others." As a result, many Christians believe that anything beyond the act of evangelism is off-limits. Some won't even go that far, and many won't engage in politics what-so-ever. I have news for those folks. Every time a legislature enacts legislation, it is an imposition of morality.

Laws against stealing impose the morality of the honest over the dishonest. Laws against prostitution impose a sexual morality. When we declare anything legal or illegal it is a statement of morality. Legislation is built upon morality and morality is built upon religious belief.

Founding Father, John Adams, who was also

America's second president, stated: "We have no government armed with power capable of contending with human passions unbridled by morality and religion...Our constitution was made for a moral and religious people. It is wholly inadequate to the government of any other."

Even Franklin and Jefferson, our least religious Founding Fathers, supported the need for a civil and virtuous people influenced by faith. A moral population built upon religion and voting our values.

Christians, in democratic countries, have been granted the freedom to choose leaders who will advance righteousness. When you hear someone say, "God's in control no matter who gets elected." A statement like that is usually intended to ease the guilt of someone who has chosen to ignore biblical values when they vote. And while it is true that God is in control no matter what, and that He has ordained the outcome of every election, He has also ordained the means to achieve that outcome, which is you and me exercising our right and responsibility to vote.

We can't ignore the positions of individual candidates on matters like abortion, same-sex marriage, and religious rights as an election cycle approaches. Those who say Christians shouldn't try to impose their morality on the general populace should listen to the advice of the late Chuck Colson: "The popular notion that 'you can't legislate morality' is a myth. Morality is legislated every day from the vantage point of one value system being chosen over another. The question is not whether we will legislate morality, but whose morality gets legislated."

I know well that if there is anything that will spark a spontaneous debate, if not an outright argument, it's a discussion involving politics. Even among believers, not everyone agrees on every issue. As Christ followers, what should be our involvement and attitude about politics?

As far back as I can remember I've heard the age-old adage that, "religion and politics don't mix." But is that true? Let's see what the Bible says:

We are supposed to respect authority. God has His hand in politics, and He puts those in power there for a reason. We may not always understand why, but He sees the bigger picture. Romans 13:1-3 says, "Everyone must submit to governing authorities. For all authority comes from God, and those in positions of authority have been placed there by God. So, anyone who rebels against authority is rebelling against what God has instituted, and they will be punished. For the authorities do not strike fear in people who are doing right, but in those who are doing wrong. Would you like to live without fear of the authorities? Do what is right, and they will honor you." There is no doubt from this scripture that our responsibility to government is to obey the laws and be good citizens.

However, we should always put God first. Though scripture tells us to respect our leaders we can't forget who our ultimate leader is: God. God permeates and supersedes every aspect of life. God's will should take pre-eminence over everything and everyone (Matthew 6:33).

It is, in fact, God who "sets up kings and deposes them" (Daniel 2:21) because "the Most High is sovereign over the kingdoms of men and gives them to anyone He wishes" (Daniel 4:17). This means that politics is simply a method God uses to accomplish His will. And even though some men abuse their political power, meaning it for evil, in the end God means it for good, as He works "all things together for the good of those who love Him, who have been called according to His purpose" (Romans 8:28).

The only time we are to disobey the laws of men, is when those laws are at odds with the laws of God.

Acts 4:18-19 speaks of a time where leaders spoke to Peter and John and told them not to share Jesus. But Peter and John replied, "Which is right in God's eyes: to listen to you, or to Him? You be the judges! As for us, we cannot help speaking about what we have seen and heard." So, while we're told to respect our leaders, we must understand that the choices they make may sometimes go against the will of God. In these circumstances, we must listen to our ultimate leader. Peter tells us in Acts 5:29, "We must obey God rather than human beings!" At the end of the day, God is our one true ruler.

As Christians we are called to pray for our leaders, even when we don't like them, or we don't like their attitudes. 1 Timothy 2:1-4 tells us, "First of all, then, I urge that supplications, prayers, intercessions, and thanksgivings be made for all people, for kings and all who are in high positions, that we may lead a peaceful and quiet life, godly and dignified in every way. This is good, and pleases God our Savior, who wants all people to be saved and come to a knowledge of the truth."

The church's unique, God-given purpose does not lie in political activism. Nowhere in scripture are we given the directive to spend all our energy, our time and our money in governmental affairs. Our mission is not in changing the nation through political reform, but in changing hearts through the Word of God and His saving Grace.

However, maintaining a godly society requires that Christians become involved to some degree in politics. Whether it's by praying for our leaders, exercising our right to vote, or even holding a political office, Christians should be concerned about how their society is ruled and their government run.

What Does God Think About Abortion?

This is a divisive topic, but one which should be addressed for those who might be confused about how God feels concerning this issue. Admittedly, even some Christians struggle with this one. Since abortion is no longer "against the law" in this country (and hasn't been since the Roe v Wade decision in 1973) some are hard pressed to find fault with the topic, hence the ongoing need to educate on what God's Word says about touchy subjects such as abortion and euthanasia. God is the giver of life. He is also the determiner of when that natural life shall end.

As I've said previously, sometimes it isn't as

easy as what our own opinion might be on a particular subject. Remember in Acts 5:29 we were told that we must obey God rather than human beings, even if that means going against the law of the land. For the Christian, God's law always supersedes man's law, in all things. That can be a difficult concept for one who perhaps didn't grow up with a stellar spiritual childhood and wants to obey the man-made laws of the land.

Am I telling you that you should not obey the laws of man? Well, if you are a follower of Christ and those man-made laws are in direct opposition to the laws of God, then, as hard as it is to imagine, yes that is exactly what I am saying. I would tell you without flinching, not ever to perform an abortion, or to get an abortion, even if the law of man tells you that it is okay to do so, because taking a life is most definitely against God's will.

This is a perfect example of why Christians should be more involved in making policy for our nation. Perhaps then those moral values of the nation would more closely mimic God's will, and we wouldn't run into these sticky issues.

Just as we must tell people not to murder in other scenarios, not to steal, lie or commit adultery among other things (even creating laws to this effect), it is always important to look at the Biblical context of issues such as these.

Something does not have to be "against the law" in order to be wrong. Sometimes a thing is against God's law, or His will, even if man has passed laws protecting that morally wrong issue. Culture has given in to societal pressure in numerous areas, permitting certain things that would have been viewed as abhorrent even twenty-five years ago, all in the name of "progressivism". That doesn't mean God has changed His mind on the subject. God gives life and His view on life has not changed. Hebrews 13:8 says, "Jesus Christ is the same yesterday and today and forever."

By the way, I personally don't believe killing babies is progressive at all. Rather, it dates us back to a time when savagery ruled the land and babies were offered up to Moloch (a false Canaanite god). During Biblical times followers of Moloch would place their babies into the red-hot metal hands of this false idol, to be burned to death in sacrifice to their god, supposedly to garner favor with this monster. It hurts my heart to think of a parent willingly placing their child in harm's way, whether it be into the hands of an idol, or into the hands of an abortionist.

Actually, and this fact has been pointed out to me by a person intent on 'proving me wrong', the word 'abortion' never appears in the Bible. I am and have always been aware of this. There are lots of words used in modern English that don't appear in the Bible.

That is an easy one to explain. If a word was not commonly in use during the period in which a piece of scripture was inspired by God and written down, it stands to reason that word would not be used in the ancient text. Let's use common sense when viewing these subjects. The reader would have been thoroughly confused by an unfamiliar word appearing in their Holy text. I would think that for most people, at least those who place any value at all on human life, "thou shalt not murder" should be a sufficient terminology and command.

On the word abortion not appearing in scripture, however, just because that word isn't used in the Bible, doesn't mean that God's Word is silent on the subject. On the contrary. The Word has a great deal to say about when life begins and the sanctity of that life.

Holy Scripture is very clear that the unborn child is a valuable life. King David illustrates this beautifully in Psalm 139:13-16

"For you created my inmost being. You knit me together in my mother's womb. I praise You because I am fearfully and wonderfully made;

Your works are wonderful; I know that full well. My frame was not hidden from You when I was made in the secret place, when I was woven together in the depths of the earth. Your eyes saw my unformed body; all the days ordained for me were written in Your book before one of them came to be."

So, even without the benefit of modern science (ultrasounds, OBGYNs, etc.), David put into words what the human heart knows instinctively: the unborn child is a human life.

He's not alone, by the way. Job says, "Your hands shaped me and made me. Will You now turn and destroy me? Remember that You molded me like clay...You gave me life and showed me kindness, and in Your providence watched over my spirit" (10:8-12)

The prophet Jeremiah writes, "He did not kill me in the womb; so, my mother would have been my grave" (20:17)

In Ecclesiastes we read, "As you do not know the way the spirit comes to the bones in the womb of a woman with child, so you do not know the work of God who makes everything (11:5).

In these and other verses we can see that the Bible affirms the life and value of unborn children. The Bible goes yet further explaining that unborn life is valuable because that child has been uniquely created by God. Paul declares, "He Himself gives everyone life and breath and everything else" (Acts 17:25).

According to the Bible, conception, pregnancy and birth are not distinct stages of life that can be separated to serve our own purposes. They are, instead, part of a continuum of life beginning at conception. Therefore, we read about conception (Psalms 51:5), the womb (Psalm 139:13, and birth (Luke 1:31; 2:6-7) in terms of actual life rather than the mere potential for life. Neither size of the child, nor distance from the birth canal determines life. God alone determines the instant life begins, the moment He begins the work of creating that life. And God doesn't just create human life, He is intimately and actively involved in His work.

This is verified when the Bible speaks of God knowing specific people in the womb: when Rebekah inquired of the Lord about her difficult pregnancy, she was told by God that two nations wrestled within her womb, that one would be stronger than the other and that the older would serve the younger. This was Jacob and Esau. When the time came for her to give birth twin boys were in her womb (Genesis 25:22-24).

In Jeremiah 1:5 we read that God said, "Before I formed you in the womb, I knew you, before you were born, I set you apart; I appointed you as a prophet to the nations".

In Psalm 139:16 David claims, "Your eyes saw my unformed body; all the days ordained for me were written in your book before one of them came to be". And Paul, in Galatians 1:15 says, "God, who set me apart from my mother's womb and called me by grace,"

Of John the Baptist we read, "He will be great in the sight of the Lord…and he will be filled with the Holy Spirit even before he is born." (Luke 1:15)

While it is true that none of us can claim to be The Prophet Jeremiah or Saint Paul, we can confidently know that God has a purpose for each of our lives. As Paul puts it, "From one man He made all the nations, that they should inhabit the whole earth; and He marked out their appointed times in history and the boundaries of their lands. God did this so that they would seek Him and perhaps reach out for Him and find Him." Acts 17:26-27.

Yes, God creates and values life, but the Bible won't let us stop there, He also protects and defends it. This truth resonates throughout the pages of Scripture. He thunders from the top of Mount Sinai, "You shall not murder" (Exodus 20:3).

The wise understand, "There are six things

the Lord hates, seven that are detestable to Him: haughty eyes, a lying tongue, hands that shed innocent blood... (Proverbs 6:16-19). As we study Scripture, we see a God who stands consistently ready to come to the aid of the weak and powerless. A person who has no voice is defenseless. A person who cannot protest is powerless. The unborn child has no voice and therefore cannot protest. By the grace of God, and at His command, we are their defense on earth.

I have heard multiple reasons for why someone thinks getting an abortion is okay, or even justified. Let's address a couple of those from a scientific perspective now:

*It's not really a baby, just a blob of tissue. It's just a fetus.

Scientists, (in numbers which do not match up to popular belief, at least from what we are told in the media) disagree overwhelmingly with that statement.

On Princeton University's website, www.princeton.edu, (keeping in mind that Princeton is a predominantly liberal university) we are told, their consensus is that life begins at fertilization with the Embryo's Conception.

Quoting from England: Mosby-Wolfe, 1996, p.31, "Development of the embryo begins at stage 1 when a sperm fertilizes an oocyte and together, they form a zygote."

In Keith L. Moore's 'Essentials of Human Embryology', Toronto: B.C. Decker Inc, 1988, p.2, we read, "Human development begins after the union of male and female gametes or germ cells during a process known as fertilization (conception).

Let me ask you this. If that "blob" of tissue is left alone to grow and develop to fruition, will it be a puppy, a snail, a beetle, a sea turtle, or a human child? If it were any one of these, besides the human child there would be environmental and animal cruelty laws to protect it. Sadly, statistically, in this country, the most dangerous place for a human baby has become the womb.

Many, in more recent decades, have taken to calling our unborn children fetuses. There is a logical reason for that. If they use terms like fetus, which is much less personal, more people are comfortable with the idea of that unborn child being unimportant. Fetus refers to any unborn animal in the womb, putting humans on the same level as the beasts of the field. However, if we were talking about the slaughter of millions of animals in the womb, we would likely be deafened by the outcry from those who would come forth to protect those animals. I cannot tell you how it saddens me, and I'm sure God, that the outcry for the human unborn is not nearly so loud.

*A woman should be able to do whatever she wants to do with her own body.

To a certain degree that is a true statement. However, what many people don't understand is that an unborn child's body and that mother's body are two separate entities. Though the child is within the mother's body, she is separated from it by the placenta. This baby is blessed and equipped with her own distinctive DNA, her own 23 unique pairs of chromosomes and her own blood type, which almost always deviates from that of the mother and requires a blood transfusion at birth if it does not. It is true that the child currently resides in the mother's womb, due to actions freely engaged in by that mother, but she is her own individual human being.

*What if the child was conceived by rape or incest?

According to a study from the Guttmacher Institute in New York, done in 2005, you might be surprised. The results showed that less than 1% of abortions were performed due to reasons of rape, and less than .05% for incest. Fewer than 1% said their parent's or partner's input had any bearing on their decision to abort. Using various reasons for the decision, from inconvenience, to finances, to the lack of freedom which would result from having a baby, the abortion was being used as a means of post-fertilization contraceptive measure. Keep in mind that was 15 years ago. The world has become, sadly, much more liberal since that time.

*Why would you want to bring a baby into this world, with so many unwanted children out there already? That just means more kids on the streets, or in foster care.

Were you aware that somewhere between 800,000 and 900,000 abortions are performed in America each year? Maybe you didn't know that there are up to 2,000,000 couples looking to adopt every single year as well? Only 4% of women who find themselves with an unwanted pregnancy place their children through adoption.

While you are correct that the number of homeless children in America is at an all-time high, around 2.5 million currently, most of them are not homeless alone. Due to circumstances revolving around natural disasters, parental job loss, etc., or loss of a home, the parent is homeless along with their children. This is not a situation resulting in "unwanted children", but a situation where the entire family unit needs help. More programs have been developed to help those individuals and even more are in development around the country.

The percentage of homeless kids in this country 'without parents' is relatively small and consists mostly of teens who have run away or escaped family situations which were undesirable. Many states have and are developing programs which allow these teens to access housing, medical and other needs without parental consent.

As far as foster care goes, these are children who, largely, have been removed from a household where they are considered "at risk". There are approximately 400,000 children in foster care in America. These are children whose parents are unable, currently, to care for them for a period time. For the most part, not unwanted children. Most of these kids will be placed back with their parent or parents once the courts have deemed it safe and appropriate to do so.

So, you see, claiming that abortions relieve the world of 'unwanted' homeless children and children in foster care is untrue. If a woman finds herself in an unwanted pregnancy, there are many options aside from abortion.

Now, having said all of that, if you are a person who has had an abortion, I don't want you to think there is no hope. It is not true that you have built a wall that cannot be broken down, or a vast wasteland that cannot be crossed. It is not true that your act will cause God to stop loving you. If you don't know Jesus as Lord and Savior, I implore you to reach out to Him. He has been right by your side, all along, waiting for you to stop fighting and come to Him. He is a merciful and just God, and He loves you. I mean REALLY loves you. If you were the only human being on earth, He would have died on that cross for you alone. Admit that you are a sinner (just like the rest of us must do by the way) and ask for His forgiveness. I assure you that His forgiveness will envelope you and give you a peace that boggles the mind, the moment those words leave your mouth. Ask Him into your heart and let Him lead you into all righteousness. That is one decision you will never ever regret.

How Does God Feel About Homosexuality?

Another touchy and controversial subject. Wow, what did I get myself into here? Yet, another topic for which questions arise on an almost daily basis. This, as our current culture becomes more welcoming of whatever society deems acceptable now.

Meanwhile, media, government and our children's classrooms are fraught with dangerous forms of "progressive thinking" and new rules about political correctness, which are beaten into our collective heads and everyday lives non-stop. All of this to the point that to quote the Bible or express one's own opinion is often touted as a hate crime.

Well, let me say first that as Christians we are commanded to LOVE everyone, no matter their faults or differences. Let's face it, we all have our faults and Jesus loves us anyway, doesn't He? I don't have a problem loving everyone. But I certainly don't like everything they do (sin), and I will not be bullied into thinking that I am a hateful person because I believe in the inerrant Word of God and express my own opinion on any given subject. I'm in good company there, because God hates sin too, but He loves us despite it and even grants us grace when we don't deserve it, just for humbling ourselves and asking Him to forgive us and cover us with His amazing grace and mercy.

All this political correctness and anti-biblical

progressive thinking is working to remove morality from the fabric of our culture and is attempting to further shape the way we live in a way that I'm sure breaks the Lord's heart.

I want to make something abundantly clear. The Bible says that homosexuality and sexual impurity are wrong (sin), so I believe that too. The very clear language in the Word of God leaves me no choice but to hold this opinion. We used to be able to express our own thoughts and biblical world perspective without being attacked. That is not so anymore. However, I would rather stand with God and have people condemn me, than stand with people and have God condemn me, so my opinion will not change no matter the attacks from those who don't value the sovereignty of God's Word.

I could not claim to be a follower of Christ, if I did not follow Christ and the infallible, inerrant Word of God on every issue. God's Word isn't a list of ideas that we can pick and choose from by deciding which bits of scripture we will follow and which we will ignore. To do so would sometimes, admittedly, be easier, but we as Christians were not promised easy. If you are looking to be winner of your local popularity contest these days, choosing Christianity might not be the easiest way to get there.

Jesus said, in John 15:18-21, If the world hates you, know that it has hated Me before it hated you. If you were of the world, the world would love you as its own; but because you are not of the world, but I chose you out of the world, Therefore the world hates you. Remember the

Word that I said to you. A servant is not greater than its master. If they persecuted me, they will also persecute you. If they kept My word, they will also keep yours. But all these things they will do to you on account of My Name, because they do not know Him who sent Me."

While the Bible is clear that sexual impurity is sin, I do admit to becoming increasingly frustrated with people who try to make homosexuality "the worst sin" a human being can commit. The Bible is clear about how God sees sin, ALL sin. In the Old Testament sins were listed, graded and prescribed punishments, depending on the severity of the sin, but salvation through Christ came to us when Jesus hung on the cross, died, and rose again, if we simply confess Him as Lord and Savior.

As a matter of fact, though God hates sin, He hates self-righteousness even more. Isaiah 64:6 tells us, "We have all become like one who is unclean, and all our righteous deeds are like a polluted garment (in the KJ version, "filthy rags"). We all fade like a leaf, and our iniquities, like the wind, take us away."

The moment you begin to think of yourself "more" than someone else (you know what I mean, better, holier, more worthy) you become "less" in the eyes of God. Matthew 23:11-12, "The greatest among you shall be your servant. Whoever exalts himself will be humbled, and whoever humbles himself will be exalted."

There are 613 laws and commands in the Bible's Old Testament scriptures. Read James 2:10, it tells us that according to God's law, if you have offended in even one of those laws or commandments you have broken them all, whew! Sin is sin and we are all guilty. Praise God for the sacrifice of a perfect Jesus to release us from the pain of the death we deserve to the beauty of eternity with the Father by simply confessing Jesus as the Son of God and inviting Him into our hearts forever.

In the New Testament, if we declare that Jesus is the Son of God, turn from our wicked ways and ask Jesus to be our Savior, He will forgive us of our sin. We are forgiven no matter what the wrong we've committed was. Grace. Freely given.

For those who wonder, there is only one unpardonable sin, which I will address in a later chapter. So, now that I have probably angered both those who think being gay is the worst sin in the universe and those who are gay or have a family member or friend who is gay, let me remind you again that God says we are ALL imperfect. Have you ever lied? How about taking something that didn't belong to you, even something small like a pen or a paper clip? Have you ever gossiped, taken the Lord's name in vain or cussed someone out? How about hate? Do you have an anger problem, or drink too much? Have you ever lusted after another person, even if it was just in your mind? Have you ever wished harm or death on another? What about forgiveness? Do you have a problem with forgiving or asking for forgiveness, even if THEY started it? All of these and many more are on that list of sins. We have ALL sinned and fallen short of the glory of God. So, we all need Jesus in our lives. Yes, we

ALL need His grace and forgiveness.

Now, I also understand that no one likes to have their sin pointed out to them (the whole speck in your brother's eye and plank in your own scenario in Matthew 7:5). There are things which were done to me as a child and as a young woman that still creep into my dreams at night and attempt to haunt me even now. People that it took me many years to forgive. And though I have learned to live with those things, I still struggle with thoughts of being dirty to the core and having to remind myself of whose child I am now, only by His grace.

I have also done things in my past that I was ashamed of and have had to throw myself on the mercy of the Lord, asking for His forgiveness, while simultaneously not accepting that grace which He offered, for a very long time, (because I knew deep in my heart, I didn't really deserve it). Learning to forgive myself has been a harder struggle than forgiving others, but I'm getting there. However, I am abundantly aware of the fact that I am only free because of the sacrifice of Jesus Christ. I am the last person in the world who will ever claim to be better than anyone else. Not a better person or a better Christian.

In researching the Word concerning the subject of homosexuality and sexual impurity I found seven scriptures in the Old Testament that are clear about where God stands on this subject. But before you say, "See, it is only mentioned in the Old Testament and doesn't apply to Christians today", I also found 4 scriptures in the New Testament that are abundantly clear.

Let us see what God's Word says about the subject of Homosexuality and sexual impurity. Then I will leave you to talk it over with God. He still listens and He still answers prayers.

Old Testament:

Genesis 19:1-11, ""That evening the two angels came to the entrance of the city of Sodom. Lot was sitting there, and when he saw them, he stood up to meet them. Then he welcomed them and bowed with his face to the ground. "My lords," he said, "come to my home to wash your feet, and be my guests for the night. You may then get up early in the morning and be on your way again." "Oh no," they replied. "We'll just spend the night out here in the city square." But Lot insisted, so at last they went home with him. Lot prepared a feast for them, complete with fresh bread made without yeast, and they ate. But before they retired for the night, all the men of Sodom, young and old, came from all over the city and surrounded the house. They shouted to Lot, "Where are the men who came to spend the night with you? Bring them out to us so we can have sex with them!" So, Lot stepped outside to talk to them, shutting the door behind him. "Please, my brothers," he begged, "don't do such a wicked thing. Look, I have two virgin daughters. Let me bring them out to you, and you can do with them as you wish. But please, leave these men alone, for they are my guests and are under my protection. "Stand back!" they shouted. "This fellow came to town as an outsider, and now he's acting like our judge! We'll treat you far worse than those other men!" And they lunged toward Lot to break down the door. But the two angels reached out, pulled Lot into the house, and bolted the door. Then they blinded all the men, young and old, who were at the door of the house, so they gave up trying to get inside."

Leviticus 18:22,"Do not practice homosexuality, having sex with another man as with a woman. It is a detestable sin."

Leviticus 20:13,"If a man practices homosexuality, having sex with another man as with a woman, both men have committed a detestable act. They must both be put to death, for they are guilty of a capital offense."

Judges 19:16-24, "That evening an old man came home from his work in the fields. He was from the hill country of Ephraim, but he was living in Gibeah, where the people were from the tribe of Benjamin. When he saw the travelers sitting in the town square, he asked them where they were from and where they were going. "We have been in Bethlehem in Judah," the man replied. "We are on our way to a remote area in the hill country of Ephraim, which is my home. I traveled to Bethlehem, and now I'm returning home. But no one has taken us in for the night, even though we have everything we need. We have straw and feed for our donkeys and plenty of bread and wine for ourselves. "You are welcome to stay with me," the old man said. "I will give you anything you might need. But whatever you do, don't spend the night in the square." So, he took them home with him and fed the donkeys. After they washed their feet, they ate and drank together. While they were enjoying themselves, a crowd of troublemakers from the town surrounded the house. They began beating at the door and shouting to the old man, "Bring out the man who is staying with you so we can have sex with him." The old man stepped outside to talk to them. "No, my brothers, don't do such an evil thing. For this man is a guest in my house, and such a thing would be shameful. Here, take my virgin daughter and this man's concubine. I will bring them out to you, and you can abuse them and do whatever you like. But don't do such a shameful thing to this man."

1 Kings 14:24, "And there were also male cult prostitutes in the land. They did according to all the abominations of the nations that the LORD drove out before the people of Israel."

1 Kings 15:12, "He put away the male cult

prostitutes out of the land and removed all the idols that his fathers had made."

2 Kings 23:7, "He also tore down the living quarters of the male and female shrine prostitutes that were inside the Temple of the LORD, where the women wove coverings for the Asherah pole."

New Testament:

Romans 1:18-32, "But God shows his anger from heaven against all sinful, wicked people who suppress the truth by their wickedness.... Yes, they knew God, but they wouldn't worship him as God or even give him thanks. And they began to think up foolish ideas of what God was like. As a result, their minds became dark and confused. Claiming to be wise, they instead became utter fools. And instead of worshiping the glorious, ever-living God, they worshiped idols made to look like mere people and birds and animals and reptiles. So, God abandoned them to do whatever shameful things their hearts desired. As a result, they did vile and degrading things with each other's bodies. They traded the truth about God for a lie. So, they worshiped and served the things God created instead of the Creator himself, who is worthy of eternal praise! Amen. That is why God abandoned them to their shameful desires. Even the women turned against the natural way to have sex and instead indulged in sex with each other. And the men, instead of having normal sexual relations with women, burned with lust for each other. Men did shameful things with other men, and as a result of this sin, they suffered within themselves the penalty they deserved. Since they thought it foolish to acknowledge God, he abandoned them to their foolish thinking and let them do things that should never be done. Their lives became full of every kind of wickedness, sin, greed, hate, envy, murder, quarreling, deception, malicious behavior, and gossip. They are backstabbers, haters of God, insolent, proud, and boastful. They invent new ways of sinning, and they disobey their parents. They refuse to understand, break their promises, are heartless, and have no mercy. They know God's justice requires that those who do these things deserve to die, yet they do them anyway. Worse yet, they encourage others to do them, too."

1 Corinthians 6:9-11, "Don't you realize that those who do wrong will not inherit the Kingdom of God? Don't fool yourselves. Those

who indulge in sexual sin, or who worship idols, or commit adultery, or are male prostitutes, or practice homosexuality, or are thieves, or greedy people, or drunkards, or are abusive, or cheat people-none of these will inherit the Kingdom of God. Some of you were once like that. But you were cleansed; you were made holy; you were made right with God by calling on the name of the Lord Jesus Christ and by the Spirit of our God."

1 Timothy 1:8-10, "Now we know that the law is good, if one uses it lawfully, understanding this, that the law is not laid down for the just but for the lawless and disobedient, for the ungodly and sinners, for the unholy and profane, for those who strike their fathers and mothers, for murderers, the sexually immoral, men who

practice homosexuality, enslavers, liars, perjurers, and whatever else is contrary to sound doctrine ...."

Jude 7, "And don't forget Sodom and Gomorrah and their neighboring towns, which were filled with immorality and every kind of sexual perversion. Those cities were destroyed by fire and serve as a warning of the eternal fire of God's judgment."

Now, here I will touch on a practical point to heterosexuality. We were designed, man and woman, to procreate. To multiply and fill the earth. God gave man "seed" by which to procreate. God considered the "seed" to be very important. That seed was not to be wasted. If you read the Scripture in Genesis 38:9, you will see that when Omar spilled his seed on the ground,

God was so angered that He slew him. We also read in Scripture that man's waste was considered more impure than the waste of animals. Special places outside of the camp were designed in which man was to defecate. He was to dig a hole first and empty his waste into the hole. Conversely, animal waste was used as fertilizer and was not considered to pollute the ground. Can you imagine God's sadness at seeing the seed He considers so important being discarded by emptying it into an impure receptacle, a place from where human waste proceeds? Just one more thing to think about.

Remember that we are all sinners in need of God's forgiveness and grace. None better than another in His eyes. If you know you are an imperfect human being, like me, and you are looking for a God who is bigger than your sin, His Name is Jesus. Come home.

How Many Genders Did God Create?

Again, boy-oh-boy I'm going to get some backlash from this one, aren't I? Yet, all things considered, the truth needs to be told. Remember that I am approaching and answering every question in this book from a biblical perspective and from the wisdom contained within the infallible, inerrant Word of God, so please bear with me.

A conversation I had recently:

Her: "If God is both genders, shouldn't all people be free to choose their own gender identity?"

Me: "I'm not sure I understand the question.

What do you mean when you say that God is both genders?"

Her: "Let me explain what I mean. Focus on the Family claims its views on gender identity are based on the Scripture verse that says, "God created man in His own image" then goes on to say that this "image" includes "male and female." So, doesn't this mean God is androgynous? You know, male and female at the same time? Wouldn't this mean that humans being made "in His image" should have the right to be male or female, or even male and female if they choose?"

Me: "Hmmm, you've raised a very interesting question. I would say this is the kind of question that requires some serious thinking about the nature of God and the deeper study for meaning of a familiar biblical text. You know it really isn't surprising that we should find this subject – maleness and femaleness as "elements" or "aspects" of the image of God in man – a bit confusing. Even the Bible describes it as a great mystery. What I mean by that is that this is a "revealed truth" which must be embraced by faith since it defies analysis and comprehension by our human minds."

I went on from there to explain:

The Scripture you are referring to is Genesis 1:27 where we read, "So God created man in His own image; in the image of God, He created him; male and female He created them." If you examine this verse you will see it does NOT say that God is "androgynous." Exactly the opposite. The writer makes an important two-sided distinction using the pronouns he chooses.

The first pronoun is singular: "in the image of God He created *him*." The second is plural: "male and female He created *them*." In this we discover a significant truth. If we view the terms in the *Godward* relation, then "man" or "mankind" is one, as in all of us, men and women alike, are created equally "in His image" (read Galatians 3:28). However, amongst ourselves we are differentiated by sex as a race. We are divided into two groups, if you will, or component parts – male and female. When we read the text properly, as you can see, the meaning becomes clearer.

Now, concerning God, the fact of the matter is that though He is referred to as The Father, He is neither male nor female. He simply transcends all such categories, just as He transcends time and space concepts. The notion of an "androgynous"

God isn't just foreign, but offensive, to orthodox Christian theology.

It is we who are marked and set apart from one another in terms of sex, not God. Genesis 1:27 shows us that it is only when these two distinct halves of humanity *come together* that the image of 'God in man' is most fully revealed.

Here is where we run up against the great "mystery" of this doctrine. The Bible doesn't envision this *coming together* between the sexes as taking place within a single "androgynous" individual after all, but rather in the sacred one-flesh union of marriage.

Somehow or other (through spiritual means beyond my comprehension) it is within that sacred bond between *husband and wife* that the true stamp of God's character and the meaning of His Trinitarian essence comes through most clearly.

So, what is the world saying on this subject?

According to 'The Australian Sex Survey', published in March of 2020 the acronym "LGBT" which was once considered sufficient to represent all non-heterosexual and gender types, might need to add a few more letters. This survey listed a surprising 33 options under the question "Which of the following terms do you feel best describes your gender?" These include, but are not limited to, "gender fluid" and "Neutrois". But that's nothing, here in the U.S. we have come up with a whopping 64.

Around the world we are witnessing a social revolution in which a media frenzy centers around gender fluidity. The advocates of this rebellion insist that gender is indeterminate and must be the choice of an individual. However, scientific reality (male or female) is determined at the instant of conception, by either the presence (male) or absence (female) of the Y chromosome. That isn't a choice, but a scientific, unchangeable fact.

It is true that with the entrance of sin and its consequences into the world in the Garden of Eden that there are gender disorders of various types, just as there are abnormalities, illnesses and disabilities of all kinds present in this sinful world. And people affected by such disorders should absolutely receive compassion and support. But it is another matter when our society convinces others, including children, to enter gender/sexual experimentation, leading to inner confusion and turmoil.

One pediatrician, in a report published in 2017, described these efforts as "large scale child abuse." In their seminal 2016 report on "Sexuality and Gender," the highly respected scholars L.W. Mayer and P.R. McHugh stated, "We are concerned by the increasing tendency toward encouraging children with gender identity issues to transition to their preferred gender through medical and then surgical procedures." They concluded, "The scientific evidence...suggests we take a skeptical view toward the claim that sex-reassignment procedures provide the hoped-for benefits or resolve the underlying issues that contribute to elevated mental health risks among the transgender population."

In a report from September 2018: Harrowing statistics from a study recently published by the American Academy of Pediatrics revealed alarming levels of attempted suicide among transgender youth -- with the highest rates among transgender boys and non-binary youth.

More than half of transgender male teens who participated in the survey reported attempting suicide in their lifetime, while 29.9 percent of transgender female teens said they had attempted suicide. Among non-binary youth, 41.8 percent of respondents stated that they had attempted suicide at some point in their lives. Though suicide is the second largest cause of death in young people between the ages of 10 and 24, these rates among transgender youth are up to five times higher than those of heterosexual youth. Obviously, there are factors at work in these young minds that question the radical choices being made which can then lead to tragic consequences.

Attempting to switch or neutralize gender simply perverts God's original "very good" creation (laid out in the book of Genesis) and leads to many unnecessary problems.

Genesis 1:26-27, "Then God said, "Let us make man in our image, after our likeness. And let them have dominion over the fish of the sea and over the birds of the heavens and over the livestock and over all the earth and over every creeping thing that creeps on the earth." So, God created man in His own image, in the image of God He created him; male and female He created them." There are two sexes, male and female.

I for one care more for what God says than the opinions of man. Each person is entitled to his or her own opinion. However, no one is entitled to make up their own version of the facts and biology is biology regardless of opinion. So, reality is what it is, and the biggest reality is that God loved us so much that He sent His Son to die for us on the cross, that to believe in His Sonship and ask Him to redeem you will result in a home with Him forever, no matter your previous faults or failings.

What About Marriage. Does God Care Who We Marry?

The short answer to this one is, yes. And I will say something here which might sound very old fashioned. Marriage was created by God for the purpose of procreation. Two males cannot procreate, two females cannot procreate, a human and an animal cannot procreate, therefore, there is no point except that which is presented by lust. In Genesis 1:28, we see that God was specific. "And God blessed them. And God said to them, "Be fruitful and multiply and fill the earth and subdue it and have dominion over the fish of the sea and over the birds of the heavens and over every living thing that moves on the earth."

He created man and woman. He intended that they be together as one-unit to multiply and care for the earth God gave them as a habitation. We don't always do the very best at that but using the gifts He has given us in a perverted manner is simply a recipe for disaster.

As the apostle Paul writes, "For this reason a man shall leave his father and mother and be joined to his wife, and the two shall become one flesh.' This is a great mystery, but I speak concerning Christ and the church" (Ephesians 5:31, quoting Genesis 2:24).

Heterosexual marriage then, is the point, or *par excellence*, of the image of God in man. The place where biological beginning and spirit meet. This is the reason why it is so important to maintain the distinction between male and female the way it was designed and implemented by the creator.

A little instruction is also warranted for Christians as well. Be careful when selecting the person, you will spend the rest of your life with. Sadly, over the past decades, divorce rates among Christians have risen to mirror those of non-Christians. God does not want us to put ourselves in those positions. There is excellent advice in the pages of the Bible regarding choosing a mate and having a successful, joy filled marriage. One Scripture which is especially helpful in making that final decision is:

2 Corinthians 6:14, "Do not be unequally yoked with unbelievers. For what partnership has righteousness with lawlessness? Or what

fellowship has light with darkness?"

Yes, God cares who we marry. His desire is that we would marry another believer and spend our lives together worshipping and serving Him. Ideally, we would present to the world a unified ministry which would share Jesus with all of creation.

What is the Unpardonable Sin?

Okay, here is the answer I promised earlier on:

I don't know about you, but I spent most of my life sure that I had committed sins that were unredeemable. If, like me, you were led to believe that you could do things which would cause you to lose your salvation, you were probably just as worried as I was. I have been asked this question thousands of times, over the years, by those who worried they'd transgressed to a point of no return, and by those who wanted to hold power over another by way of their sin.

Let me help you to rest a little easier. The one and only sin for which there is no forgiveness is the ultimate blaspheming of the Holy Spirit. Many have said that this would be to use the Name of God in a profane manner. This is not what committing the ultimate blasphemy of the Holy Spirit means.

So, what does it mean? It means that we have been offered a gift by the Father. That gift is this: That God became man, came to earth, died on a cross for our sins, yours, mine, all our sins, past, present and future. That He rose again from the grave, overcoming death. That if we desire forgiveness here in this life and a place beside Him in heaven when we leave this place, we must confess that Jesus Christ is the Son of God, and that He died for "me". We must, in fact, **believe**. In so doing we accept the Father's eternal gift of the indwelling of the Holy Spirit.

Therefore, to refuse that gift, to deny Jesus as Savior and to spurn that life offered through the Holy Spirit, is to blaspheme the Holy Spirit. I find this very profound, that the only way to cause God to be so angry with you that you are denied forgiveness, is to reject His forgiveness. How ironic then that some would make statements such as: "If your God is so loving, how can He deny heaven to anyone?" When in fact, the only way you are denied eternal life with Jesus, is by refusing the Gospel of Jesus. So, don't commit the unforgiveable sin. Believe the Gospel of Christ and be saved.

Now, how do we know that blaspheming of the Holy Spirit is the unpardonable sin? Let us do a little research in God's Word, shall we?

In Matthew 12:22-32 we read, "Then they

brought him a demon-possessed man who was blind and mute, and Jesus healed him, so that he could both talk and see. All the people were astonished and said, "Could this be the Son of David?" But when the Pharisees heard this, they said, "It is only by Beelzebub, the prince of demons, that this fellow drives out demons." Jesus knew their thoughts and said to them, "Every kingdom divided against itself will be ruined, and every city or household divided against itself will not stand. If Satan drives out Satan, he is divided against himself. How then can his kingdom stand? And if I drive out demons by Beelzebub, by whom do your people drive them out? So then, they will be your judges. But if it is by the Spirit of God that I drive out demons, then the kingdom of God has come upon you.

"Or again, how can anyone enter a strong man's house and carry off his possessions unless he first ties up the strong man? Then he can plunder his house. "Whoever is not with me is against me, and whoever does not gather with me scatters. And so, I tell you, every kind of sin and slander can be forgiven, **but blasphemy against the Holy Spirit will not be forgiven**. Anyone who speaks a word against the Son of Man will be forgiven, **but anyone who speaks against the Holy Spirit will not be forgiven, either in this age or in the age to come**."

Luke 12:9-10, "But anyone who denies me here on earth will be denied before God's angels. Anyone who speaks against the Son of Man can be forgiven, **but anyone who blasphemes the Holy Spirit will not be forgiven**."

John 3:36, "**Whoever believes in the Son has eternal life, but whoever rejects the Son will not see life,** for God's wrath remains on them."

Mark 16:16, "Whoever believes and is baptized will be saved, **but whoever does not believe will be condemned.**"

John 3:16, "For God so loved the world that he gave his one and only Son, that **whoever believes in him shall not perish but have eternal life.**"

John 3:18, "Whoever believes in him is not condemned, but whoever does not believe stands condemned already because they have not believed in the name of God's one and only Son."

So, when you find yourself in a place where you wonder if you've committed a sin that God will never forgive, remember this:

1 John 1:9, "But if we confess our sins to him, he is faithful and just to forgive us our sins and to cleanse us from all wickedness."

Psalm 103:12, "As far as the east is from the west, so far has he removed our transgressions from us."

2 Chronicles 7:14, "If my people, who are called by my name, will humble themselves and pray and seek my face and turn from their wicked ways, then I will hear from heaven, and I will forgive their sin and will heal their land."

Proverbs 28:13, "Whoever conceals their sins does not prosper, but the one who confesses and renounces them finds mercy."

If someone asks you, "Did I commit the unforgivable sin?" You may reliably say, "The fact that you asked this question tells me no you did not. A Christian cannot commit the unpardonable sin. If you committed it, you wouldn't be a Christian."

Once you are His, you are His forever!

John 10:28, "I give them eternal life, and they shall never perish; no one will snatch them out of my hand."

2 Corinthians 5:17, "Therefore, if anyone is in Christ, the new creation has come. The old has gone, the new is here!"

Is the Bible True and Reliable?

There is great information concerning this question at (answers in genesis.org). I also found lots of wonderful insight while reading Josh McDowell's book "The New Evidence That Demands a Verdict". While Atheists and skeptics alike have claimed over the centuries that the Bible is filled with errors and fairy tales, it seems this is not the case at all. I would guess the naysayers are simply louder than believers (sadly) and get more media attention than those who would defend the Bible. In gleaning answers to this question, we will first look at the spiritual dimensions. But I have also included some undisputed and compelling scientific FACTS for those of you who are hesitant to believe biblical answers on this subject.

So, can we prove the Bible is true? Jesus Christ and His disciples went about fearlessly proclaiming God's Word. Why were they so bold? They knew without a doubt the power and absolute trustworthiness of every word in scripture. They were also sure that the Holy Spirit went before them, impressing upon the hearts of hearers, the truth of His Word. For true believers this answer, though short, will be enough.

For doubters we will take the answer to this question several steps further. First, we must understand the Bible is true because it is from the author of truth, not because of some human way of defining proof. But how can we, as mere

GOD?

humans, know this for sure? Let's say you are sharing the Gospel with someone and out of the blue they ask you, "How do you know the Bible is true?" How would you answer?

If you've done much reading on the subject (as I have done), you've undoubtedly come across long lists of 'proofs' as I did (gosh there are many great ones out there - archaeological discoveries of various sorts that line up with biblical text, amazing prophecies that have come true while the world watches and other such human ways of making this point). However, our emphasis should never be on human proof, if the truth of the Word is to be our guide, Jesus Christ's own conversations with non-believers shed light on the correct approach.

His responses were often surprising, but if

we read carefully, we can see that His goal was to honor God's Word while exposing the pride and failure of hearers to submit their hearts to the Father's unquestionable authority. False pride and human ego can be enormous stumbling blocks to a real relationship with the Father. When Scripture tells us that, "pride goes before a fall", this is the lack of humility example which drives the point home. Humans want to be "their own boss" if you know what I mean.

The Bible doesn't give us a one-size-fits-all formula for defending itself, but it does give us all the guidelines we need. And in 2 Timothy 3:16-17 we see that we can be assured of its absolute authenticity. That scripture reads, "All Scripture is breathed out by God and profitable for teaching, for reproof, for correction, and for training in righteousness, that the man of God may be competent, equipped for every good work."

We must understand that the root problem is not ignorance but unbelief. God tells us in specific terms that the barrier to believing is not in the nonbeliever's view of the book; it's in their view of the Author of the book.

All people already know of God in the depths of their spirit, whether they choose to admit it or not, because He is clearly seen in the evidence of His creation. His moral law is written on their hearts. Read Roman's 1:19-20, "For what can be known about God is plain to them, because God has shown it to them. For His invisible attributes, namely His eternal power and divine nature, have been clearly perceived, ever since the creation of the world, in the things that have been made, so they are without excuse."

This is one of the areas where my husband and I have debated over the years. He is a great Bible 'apologist' and a firm believer that if he can just show a nonbeliever enough 'solid proof' they will be compelled to become believers. I on the other hand believe that faith is a huge factor in the process. I have come to realize most people enter a conversation about biblical truth with pre-conceived notions. If they are not open to "the Truth" there will not be enough proof in the world to convince them. On the other hand, if they are believers, no one with any argument to the contrary will ever be able to dissuade them from "the Truth".

Prideful hearts have no desire to submit to

the Truth. God calls those hearts "rebellious". I have an example for you: My husband and I were having a conversation with a member of one of our previous churches. We were talking about God parting the Red Sea to allow Moses and his people to cross on dry land. This member said that he didn't believe it was the Red Sea that God parted, but a connecting body of water called the "reed" sea. My husband said, "What do you find harder to believe? That God parted the Red Sea and the children of Israel crossed on dry land, or that Pharaoh and his vast army of soldiers, every single one, along with chariot horses, drowned in about 3 feet of water? Either way, and we believe it was the way the Bible indicates, the army was defeated, and the Israelites were saved."

When people reject the Bible's historical

accounts of Creation and a global Flood, for instance, Peter tells us they are "willfully" ignorant, 2Peter 3:5, "For they deliberately overlook this fact, that the heavens existed long ago and the earth was formed out of water and through water by the Word of God,". So, it isn't a matter of evidence, how little or how much; they simply don't want to be convinced.

When we look at things from this perspective, we can see that the main problem is not a lack of knowledge. Your hearer has a heart problem. He, or She has rejected the God of the Bible even before they begin to consider whether His Word could be true.

We should rely on God's Spirit and God's Word to convince hearers. Understand that modern "intellectuals" are no different from the proud Greeks of Paul's day. Scripture tells us that they lived, "in the futility of their thinking." They were, "darkened in their understanding... because of the blindness of their heart" (Ephesians 4:17-18).

Okay, so how do you break through the darkness? Know that it is not enough to demolish their wrong thinking by cold, hard logic. I've tried that. It doesn't work. Blind men cannot see the Truth, except with new sight, which can only be given through the Holy Spirit (I Corinthians 2:14).

Thank goodness, God's Spirit has already been at work convicting sinners of their unbelief, using His Word as His main tool. I've found that by relying on the Scripture's own claims, instead of my own wisdom or "clever" arguments, God empowers His own words to convict hearts and point them to Christ Jesus, see John 16:12-15 and then Hebrews 4:12, which says, "For the Word of God is living and active, sharper than any two-edged sword, piercing to the division of soul and of spirit, of joints and of marrow, and discerning the thoughts and intentions of the heart."

Knowing this, the apostle Paul did not rely on "persuasive words of human wisdom" to overwhelm his listeners with intellectual arguments, which they may not even grasp (1 Corinthians 2:4). Instead, Paul spoke plainly to his listeners "in demonstration of the Spirit and of power, that their faith should not be in the wisdom of men but in the power of God" (1 Corinthians 2:5).

God truly isn't demanding 'blind faith'. Our faith in His Word is reasonable because we live in a world created by the same almighty God who is the author of the Bible. Proof of His presence and the reliability of His Word surrounds us everywhere we turn. We can't swing a cat without hitting it. We can't walk five feet without bumping into it. In fact, once you 'know' and understand the Truth, it is the only logical choice available. Explaining this simple fact is the secret to a biblical defense of the Bible. Jesus Himself indicated that the Bible gives enough information so that everyone can know the Truth. No other resource is better. "If they do not hear Moses and the prophets," Jesus said to His Jewish listeners, "neither will they be persuaded though one rise from the dead" (Luke 16:31).

Even though Jesus was not addressing Gentiles, His words are based on a universal truth: The Bible is – and should be – our most persuasive tool.

So, if we are still not persuaded (some people are harder to convince than others), how do we know the Bible is true? Well, my first question back to you would be, "How do we know anything is true?"

Every philosophical argument must start with presuppositions, starting points or assumptions; things that cannot be proven from anything more basic than subsequent reasoning. The Bible claims to be this ultimate standard of truth, the "Word" given by the Almighty Creator God as stated in John 17:17, "Sanctify them in the truth, Your Word is Truth."

Most people point to one of three standards: their own opinion, public consensus, or great moral literature. However, these are not options if the Bible is true.

An appeal to any other standard, such as people's opinions, automatically means you are rejecting the Bible as your ultimate standard. So, what do we logically hold up, then, as the ultimate standard? There is only one logical solution. The standard must be "self-attesting" and self-authenticating." It must speak for itself and defend itself in such a way that it passes all its own standards of truth and gives a foundation for successfully interpreting all other claims to truth.

Even before modern logicians recognized this limitation to every logical argument, God's Word had already acknowledged and solved it.

Christ Jesus, the Son of God said, "I am the Truth" (John 14:6) and "God's Word is Truth" (John 17:17). Jesus claimed to define what truth is and He said God's Word is the ultimate judge of Truth (John 12:48). No truth exists apart from Him. The Bible explains it this way, "In Him are hidden all the treasures of wisdom and knowledge" (Colossians 2:3). So, clearly, the Bible claims a heightened position as the ultimate authority. God's Word says that all standards outside of Christ are "empty", because they depend on "the tradition of men, according to the basic principles of the world, and not according to Christ" (Colossians 2:8). If the Bible appealed to any other authority, it would be denying its own authoritative place as the ultimate standard.

The only 'ultimate standard' as it turns out,

that can be logically self-authenticating, is the only one that exactly matches the unique God of the Scripture, who is holy, just, true, eternal, unchanging and "cannot lie" (Titus 1:2). Only He provides a rock-hard foundation for knowledge and attests to His own truthfulness.

God consistently appeals to His own Word as the final authority. For example, His promise to bless all nations through Abraham. How did He assure Abraham His words were true? He said, "By Myself I have sworn" (Genesis 22:16) Thereby referring to Himself as the highest court of appeals.

Logically God can appeal to nothing higher than Himself. In Hebrews 6:13 the text reads, "When God made a promise to Abraham, because He could swear by no one greater, He swore by Himself."

Later, Jesus (God in flesh) made a similar claim. When Pilate questioned Jesus' authority, He answered, appealing to His own authority: "For this cause I was born, and for this cause I have come into the world, that I should bear witness to the Truth." Then Christ added, "Everyone who is of the Truth hears My voice" (John 18:37). We should understand that no one recognizes His authority except for those who are "of the Truth" - meaning those who first and foremost listen to Him!

Pilate responded cynically, "What is Truth?" but then, having been moved by Christ's words, he told the waiting crown that he found no fault at all in Jesus. The Son of God's words had spoken effectively on His behalf.

Although God's own assertion should be the ultimate proof, He also knew there would be those who doubt, and He made allowances for that. He is God after all. He even encourages us, if we feel the need, to corroborate His testimony. Jesus knew His hearers wouldn't always accept His declarations merely on His say-so. He said, "If I bear witness of myself, my witness is not true" (John 5:31-32). This is because Jewish law requires two or three witnesses to establish the truth of a matter in court (Deuteronomy 19:15) and we know that the Lord Jesus didn't come to do away with the Law, but to fulfill it. So, as a picture of the fulfillment He would deliver, He necessarily deferred to Hebrew law.

Is it proper and biblical to seek additional evidence? God will not condemn you to hell for asking questions. He understands our spiritual blindness, especially regarding heavenly things that we can't see.

"Besides", skeptics say, "Any book inspired by a holy and righteous God should be error free, shouldn't it?" And that is precisely what we've discovered. Though these skeptics have been trying, for centuries to be frank, to find errors in biblical text, they have succeeded only in reaffirming the beauty of God's pristine Word.

The Lord talks about earthly things, which we can see, "Jesus answered Him, "Are you the teacher of Israel and yet you do not understand these things? Truly, truly I say to you, we speak of what we know, and bear witness to what we have seen, but you do not receive our testimony. If I have told you earthly things and you do not believe, how can you believe if I tell you heavenly things? No one has ascended into heaven except He who descended from heaven, the Son of Man." John 3:10-13.

The Bible is filled with specific claims about history, human nature, science, and prophecy. For instance, in Leviticus the twelfth chapter and third verse God gives the edict to circumcise baby boys on the eighth day. You might wonder what was important about the eighth day? It seems that is the day in which a newborn's vitamin K levels are at their highest. This would keep the little fellow from bleeding to death. However, the scripture doesn't tell us anything about vitamin K (we wouldn't have understood the implications way back then), it just directs Jewish parents to circumcise on the eighth day.

Considering when the Bible was written and the fact that it would be thousands of years before, in 1872, Alexander Shmidt was credited for his research into the clotting of blood (naming the enzyme prothrombin); and not until the 20th century before it was discovered that Vitamin K coupled with prothrombin causes blood clotting. How did the author of Old Testament Law know this scientific fact? Well, He is the creator of the universe after all. There are many, many scientific facts within the pages of the Bible. After all, if you think about it, God created science too.

Okay, just because the Bible gets some scientific facts correct, doesn't mean it's all true, does it? Why should we believe in the inerrancy of Scripture?

"You don't really believe the Bible is true,

do you?"

I have to say the shock on the faces of those who meet an individual who believes the Bible to be without error, though sad, is also quite amusing. So, why should we believe in the inerrancy of Scripture and why are we so sure? Are the words of the Bible truly inspired?

What do we mean when we talk about the Bible being "inspired"? That word can be misleading to some and turn into a point of contention. The term is used only once in the New Testament, and the translation has left something to be desired, so it tends to elicit some discussion. The term is found in 2Timothy 3:16 and comes from the Greek (theopneustos). The longer word is made up of two words, one being the word for God (Theos, as in theology) and the other, which refers to breath or wind (pneustos, as in pneumonia and pneumatic). It is significant that the word, when used in 2Timothy 3:16, is used passively. In other words, God did not "breathe into" (inspire) all Scripture, but "breathed out" all Scripture (expired). Therefore, this Scripture is less about how the Bible came to us and more about where, or who, it came from. The Scriptures are, in fact, God breathed.

So, how did the Bible come to us? If we turn in our Bibles to 2Peter 1:21 we find that "holy men of God spoke as they were moved by the Holy Spirit". The Greek word used here is (phero) which means to bear, or to carry. It was a familiar word Luke used of the sailing ship carried along by the wind (Acts 27:15,17). Now, the human writers of the Bible certainly used their minds.

I'm not saying they were turned into zombies and forced to transcribe biblical text without their knowledge. That is absurd. What I am saying is that the Holy Spirit carried them along in their thinking so that only His God-breathed words were recorded. Paul set the matter plainly in 1Corinthians 2:13, when he said, "These things we also speak, not in words which man's wisdom teaches but which the Holy Spirit teaches."

As Christians the word "inspiration" is so deeply embedded in our Christian language that we will likely continue to use it, but now we know what it really means. God breathed out His Word and the Holy Spirit guided the writers to put it down on paper (or papyrus) as they were led. The Bible has ONE Author and many (around 40) writers. With these two acts of God – breathing out His Word and carrying the writers along by the Holy Spirit – we can finally come to a better definition of the word inspiration:

The Holy Spirit moved men to write. He allowed them to use their own styles, cultures, gifts and character. He allowed them to write of their own experiences and express what was in their minds and hearts. However, He did not allow error to influence their writings. He overruled in the expression of thought and in the choice of words for the text. So, they recorded exactly what God wanted them to say, exactly how He wanted them to say it, in their own character, styles and languages.

So long as we give "theopneustos" its real meaning, we won't find it difficult to understand the full inerrancy of the words in the Bible.

Plenary (from the Latin, meaning 'full') and verbal (from the Latin verbum, which means 'word') inspiration means the Bible is God-given, in every part and in every single word.

So, who believes the Bible is without error (I mean other than me)? Clement of Rome in the first century wrote, "Look carefully into the Scriptures, which are the true utterances of the Holy Spirit. Observe that nothing of an unjust or counterfeit character is written in them." A century later, Irenaeus concluded, "The Scriptures are indeed perfect, since they were spoken by the Word of God and His Spirit."

This was not only the view of early church leaders but has been the consistent view of evangelicals from the ancient Vaudois people of the Piedmont Valley to the sixteenth century

Protestant Reformers across Europe and up to the present day. It is liberalism that has taken a new approach. Professor Kirsopp Lake at Harvard University admitted, "It is we (the liberals) who have departed from the tradition."

Does it matter if we, as Christians, believe the Bible to be infallible and inerrant? Of course, it does. If we believe the Bible contains errors, we will be quick to accept false scientific theories that appear to prove the Bible wrong, even when those theories are wrong in themselves. In other words, we'll allow the conclusions of science, even very bad science, to dictate the accuracy of the Word of God, instead of the Word of God dictating the truth of everything in the universe. It is called faith after all.

Alright, so even after all of that, there are still

those who say that the Bible cannot be trusted. That it was written by men, fallible men, and therefore it contains errors. These naysayers also suggest that during centuries of copying, men introduced many additional errors.

The supreme argument for the accuracy of Scripture is simply that God Himself tells us it can be trusted. We have evidence that we have in our hands exactly what God said and exactly what He wants us to have.

One such evidence that the Bible has been copied accurately in the past is shown in the discovery of the Dead Sea Scrolls. These scrolls found by a shepherd boy in 1947 are dated from 250 to 150 BC (we will touch on this more in a moment). This discovery pushed back our oldest available Scripture text almost 1000 years. And when the content of the scrolls was compared to later copies, no significant differences were found, and certainly nothing which changed the meaning of the text in any way. This means scribes had been copying with great precision for almost ten centuries. This amazing discovery moved us one millennium closer to the originals.

As with the Old Testament, archaeology continually confirms the accuracy of the New Testament historical record. Here are some assorted examples:

As you may know the account of the Roman census recorded in Luke 2 (the account of Jesus' birth) is well known. What is not so well known is that some nay-sayers assumed that a Roman emperor would never issue an order for a census where "all went to be registered, everyone to his own city". This was an issue of debate for many decades. Then, a papyrus decree was discovered in Egypt which was an order for a Roman census in Egypt at the time of Trajan in AD 104, which mirrors the order of Agustus recorded in Luke 2. The Prefect Gaius Vibius Maximus ordered all those in his area to return to their own homes for the purpose of a census.

Believe it or not, at one time there were those who claimed Pilate was not a real figure of history, because the only reference to him was made in the New Testament. This was contested and argued for decades. Then in the 1950s an inscription was found at Caesarea that dedicated a theater built by Pilot to the honor of Tiberius. Though half the stone tablet is destroyed, the rest is clear: "The Tiberius which Pontius Pilate, the Prefect of Judea dedicated." The stone had been recycled to be used as part of a stairway for the remodeled theater in the third century. (remarkable how God gets things out there in order to vindicate His Word). That's not all! The British Museum in London has on display a bronze coin minted by Pontius Pilate while he was governor of Judea; it carries the date of the 17th year of Tiberius, which would be AD 30/31 - perhaps the very year of the crucifixion of Jesus.

Dr. Luke and the Polytarchs

At the time of Paul's extensive travels, each city had its own town council, known by different titles from town to town; only a careful writer of that time would record them accurately. An example of the accuracy of Luke (the writer of Acts) as a historian was found in 1877 when a block of marble—rescued from becoming builder's rubble at Thessalonica—proved to be an inscription of the civic leaders in the city sometime in the second century. These blocks are referred to as *polytarchs*. This is the word translated as "rulers of the city" in Acts 17:6-15.

Sir William Ramsay, a bucket-and-spade archaeologist who spent decades digging around modern-day Turkey, the land of Paul's travels, was a bright man with three honorary fellowships from Oxford and nine honorary doctorates from British, Continental, and American universities. He was at one time professor at Oxford and Aberdeen universities, was awarded the Victorian medal of the Royal Geographic Society in 1906 and was a founding member of the British

Academy. He was knighted in 1906 for his service to archaeology. After a lifetime of research, this was his conclusion: "You may press the words of Luke in a degree beyond any other historian's and they stand the keenest scrutiny and the hardest treatment." He added, "Christianity did not originate in a lie; and we can and ought to demonstrate this as well as believe it."

Back to the Dead Sea Scrolls. Since their discovery these timeless treasures from Qumran have amazed scholars by their priceless insights into the preservation and proper understanding of God's infallible Word.

In 1947 this young Bedouin shepherd boy stumbled upon one of the greatest archaeological discoveries of modern times. Out of curiosity one day the lad tossed a rock into a cave opening and heard pottery shatter. This discovery led to others and between 1947 and 1956 more than 900 manuscripts were found in 11 caves around Qumran, along the northwestern shore of the Dead Sea. Over 200 of the scrolls were portions of the Bible itself, dated 250 BC – AD 68. Amazingly, every Old Testament book of the Bible except Esther was represented in the find. These are the Dead Sea Scrolls.

But why do a bunch of old scrolls matter today. Well, as modern, non-believing scholars continue their attack on the veracity of the Bible, God has given these remarkable scrolls to study and confirm our confidence in the formation, preservation, translation and interpretation of His Word. As research advances, we discover more from these treasures of ancient times.

After long delays in publication, the Dead Sea Scrolls were unveiled to the public. Manuscript 4QMMT (also known as 'Some of the Works of the Law') states, "We have written to you so that you should understand the Book of Moses and the Books of the Prophets and David." This text, dated around 150 BC, is possibly the oldest existing document referencing a closed three-part Old Testament canon. It supports the words of Jesus in Luke 24:44 when He speaks of the Old Testament as "the Law of Moses and the Prophets and the Psalms."

This text fits perfectly with the claim by the first-century historian, Josephus, that no new books were added to Scripture after the time of Ezra around 425 BC. Thus, 4QMMT is evidence that further illustrates that the Old Testament was likely fixed in Ezra's day and not by some Jewish council at Jamnia around AD 90 as was previously claimed by those seeking to discredit the Bible.

Some early scholars questioned the dates of the ancient scrolls, ascribed by paleography, which studies changes in ancient lettering over time. However, doubts were eradicated when several scrolls were carbon-14 tested in the 1990s. Of particular interest is the Great Isaiah Scroll, the only complete book of the Bible found in the caves of Qumran, which was dated to 125 BC, and confirmed by two independent tests. This example proved how reliably accurate our modern copies are.

Yes, more and more we find that archaeology supports the Bible. We are told in Psalm 85:11,

"Truth shall spring out of the earth," and in Psalm 119:89, "Forever, O Lord, Your Word is settled in heaven." God's Word is sure. It outlasts human generations, and in His own time God vindicates its truth.

Here are some additional archaeological finds that have stood the test of time:

Abraham's home city of Ur was excavated by Sir Leonard Woolley, with surprising evidence of near luxury. The customs of Patriarchal times, as described in the Bible, are endorsed by archaeological finds in such places as Ur, Mari, and Nineveh. These are actual written records from that day – not something put down in writing at some point in the distant future and they bear the marks of eyewitnesses.

The records of the five kings who fought

against four kings in Genesis 14 are very interesting, in that the names of the people concerned are the known names of those of the times written in that biblical account.

Following the discovery of the Ugaritic library, it has become clear that the Psalms of David are properly ascribed to his times and not to the Maccabean period of 800 years later as some critics claimed for countless decades. The renowned scholar William Foxwell Albright wrote, after inspecting the evidence, "To suggest that the Psalms of David should be dated to the Maccabean period is absurd."

The discovery of the entrance to the Solomonic City of Gezer provides major evidence regarding the Assyrian period.

As for King Sargon of Assyria, mentioned in

Isaiah 20:1, challenged by critics for many years, because they knew of no king named Sargon in lists of Assyrian kings. His palace has been recovered at Khorsabad, including a wall inscription and a library record endorsing the battle against the Philistine city of Ashdod, also mentioned in Isaiah 20:1. Dr. Clifford Wilson uncovered part of a pathway between Sennacherib's palace and the temple where his sons killed him. This was during a time called "The Reign of Terror" not long after Soloman's death.

We now know from the Babylonian Chronicle that the date of Nebuchadnezzar's capture of Jerusalem was the night of March 15/16 597 BC.

We also know that Belshazzar really was the king of Babylon during this time because his father Nabonidus, who was undertaking archaeological research, was away from Babylon for about 10 years. He appointed his son Belshazzar as co-regent during that time. Critics had previously said there was no such king until his palace and library were uncovered. Additionally, several prophecies against Babylon, in Jeremiah 51,52 have literally been fulfilled.

F. E. Peters states that, "on the basis of manuscript tradition alone, the works that made up the Christians' New Testament were the most frequently copied and widely circulated books of antiquity." (Peters, HH, 50) As a result, the accuracy of the New Testament text rests on a multitude of manuscript evidence. Counting Greek copies alone, the New Testament is preserved in some 5,656 partial and complete manuscript portions that were copied by hand from the second through the fifteenth centuries. (Geisler, GIB, 385) All remarkably accurate to modern text examples.

There are now more than 5,686 known Greek manuscripts of the New Testament. Add to that over 10,000 Latin Vulgate and at least 9,300 other early versions, and we have close to, if not more than, 25,000 (and counting, as new copies are found continually) full and partial manuscript copies of the New Testament in existence today. There is no other document of antiquity which comes close to such numbers and testament of accuracy.

I've always found it amazing that, in comparison, Homer's Iliad is second, with only 643 manuscripts still surviving. Yet, we don't hear of scholars out there claiming there is no 'proof' that Homer's work is authentic. Just more evidence that there are those who would try to discredit the Bible if they were able. However, it just so happens that these thousands and thousands of New Testament manuscripts, some dating as far back as within the later lifespan of the disciples themselves, are so accurate as to defy imagination. So much for those who claim, "The Bible has been changed over the years to satisfy some king's wishes and is no longer reliable." No, these early manuscripts are so close to the modern text as to be virtually identical.

Additional archaeological proofs abound. Here are some of the ones I found and there are plenty of others if you care to look. I don't have room to include them all.

James, the brother of Jesus was martyred

in AD 62. A mid first century ossuary (casket) discovered in 2002 bears this inscription: "James, son of Joseph, brother of Jesus" ("Ya'akov bar Yosef akhui di Yeshua"). The ossuary provoked much controversy, as the inscription was originally suspected of being a forgery. However, two eminent paleographers confirmed it as authentic in 2012. New Testament scholar Ben Witherington stated: "if, as seems probable, the ossuary found in the vicinity of Jerusalem and dated to about AD 63 is indeed the burial box of James, the brother of Jesus, this inscription is the most important extra-biblical evidence of its kind.

There is now evidence that Philistines had European ancestry. DNA was extracted from skeletons found at the Philistine city of

Ashkelon in modern-day Israel. The results of testing confirmed what the Bible says about the Philistines. Jeremiah 47:4 and Amos 9:7 connect the Philistines with Caphtor, which has been identified as Crete, the home of the Minoan civilization. The DNA record shows that the philistines quickly intermarried with the local population, diluting the genetic signature.

The 2018 excavation at Tel es-Safi (the Philistine city of Gath) reached a layer that dates to the 11th century BC, the time of King David. The walls of this layer are 13 feet thick, twice as thick as previously excavated walls from the 10th and 9th centuries BC. Archaeologist Aren Maier called it the "Goliath layer", after the city's most famous resident of the time.

As the Temple Mount Sifting Project

reopened in a new Jerusalem location, researchers announced the discovery of a clay seal impression (bulla), identifying it as "the first readable ancient Hebrew inscription found on the Temple Mount." The priestly family of Immer served in the temple (1Chronicles 24:14). Pashur, son of Immer, is called the chief official in the temple of Yahweh, when he had Jeremiah beaten and put in the stocks (Jeremiah 20:1-2).

A bulla (clay seal impression) was found in the Givati parking lot excavation, the largest ongoing excavation in Jerusalem (since 2007). Archaeologists recovered it from the ruins of a building that was probably destroyed during the Babylonian destruction of Jerusalem in 586 BC. In 2Kings 23:11, Nathan-Melech is described as an official in the court of King Josiah. The phrase

"Servant of the King" appears often in the Bible and on bullae.

When archaeologists discovered the New Testament-era Pool of Siloam (John 9:7) in 2004 during a sewer repair project, they also discovered the lower end of the first-century street that led up to the Temple Mount. Since then, work has been ongoing to excavate the street so that both Jewish and Christian pilgrims today can walk the same road that Jewish and Christian pilgrims walked in the first century. This underground street hasn't become entirely accessible yet, but a ceremony opening part of the street in the summer of 2018 drew the US ambassador, along with other dignitaries.

Jerusalem is a city of many names in ancient texts, and even modern times – it is known now as Jerusalem in most of the English-speaking world, Yerushalayim in Hebrew and Al-Quds in Arabic. In October of 2018, archaeologists reported that they'd found the very first instance ever of the word "Jerusalem" appearing, spelled out in full, rather than another variant. The inscription was found on a column in an ancient pottery workshop dating back around 2000 years. The workshop is near the city's modern-day International Convention Center.

I'm sure you will agree that these were wonderful examples of how archaeological digs are uncovering, day-by-day, more evidence of the truth of the Bible, however, it still all comes back to faith in the Word of God and its infallible author.

Nowhere did Christ more plainly express

His belief in the authority of Scripture than in Matthew 5:18, when He said, "For assuredly, I say to you, till heaven and earth pass away, one jot or one tittle sill by no means pass from the law till all is fulfilled." Later in His earthly ministry, Jesus applied the same authority to His own words: "Heaven and earth will pass away, but My words will by no means pass away" Matthew 24:35.

In 1972 a 'liberal' scholar, John A. T. Robinson, published a detailed study of each of the books of the New Testament and concluded that each and every one must have been completed before the year AD 70. In addition, he condemned the "sheer scholarly laziness" of those who assumed a late date for the New Testament and added, "It is sobering too to discover how little basis there is for many of the dates confidently assigned by modern experts to the New Testament documents."

I believe we may confidently conclude from all evidence shown that the Gospels and letters of the New Testament were written down by the traditionally accepted writers who lived in the first century.

As I conclude my answer to this very important question about the authenticity and reliability of the Bible, I hope you will agree that there is ample evidence as to its veracity. If this answer hasn't convinced you, then I hope you will be compelled to further investigate on your own. There are many excellent resources available online and in book form, the most important of which is God's own Word, the Holy Bible.

What is My Purpose?

Now this is a great question, one we have heard on multiple occasions from many who are seeking to know what God has in store for their lives.

We all want to know that we are making a difference. When you wake in the morning feeling purposeless it can be incredibly frustrating.

If you compare your life to the images you see on social media you can be led to believe that everyone else's lives are passionate, engaged and meaningful. It appears they all have deep relationships, rewarding jobs and a sense of direction that compels them to jump out of bed each morning ready to take on the world. Don't be fooled by the media hype.

We all want to believe God has something good in store for us, don't we? No one wants to think they have been put on this earth to live a life of painful drudgery in which every day is a total drag. After all, the Bible is full of passages about joy. While we realize that doesn't mean every single day is a circus parade in our honor, it does mean that a sense of overall gladness should permeate our lives.

In Psalm 63:7, David said, "...for You have been my help, and in the shadow of your wings I will sing for joy." Well, how can we get to that wonderful place of joy? The place where instead of wandering aimlessly through life, we are singing for joy (or at least making a joyful noise)?

I guess my first question to you would be, are you living in God's purpose? Romans 8:28

says, "And we know that for those who love God all things work together for good, for those who are called according to His purpose." So, again I will ask, are you living according to His purpose? The key point here is that we live in the purpose for which we were designed by our Creator God. If we wake each morning with ourselves on our minds, with our goals focused on things besides pleasing the Lord, then we will never feel content or fulfilled.

Why don't we look at some signs that might indicate to us whether or not we are living in God's purpose? Then we can look at some ways to turn things around to begin living a meaningful, enthusiastic, joyful life.

Before we begin, I do want to make at least one caveat. God is God and if you are a follower of Jesus, He works all things, including your life, according to His purposes. Nothing can happen without God ordaining it.

Psalm 57:2 says, "I cry out to God Most High, to God who fulfills His purpose for me." This verse is key to understanding God's purpose for our lives. He has numbered our days and will fulfill every purpose He has for us in His perfect timing.

Let's not be silly though. Obviously, our own choices and actions matter. We can choose to do the right things. Things that will give us more joy and a sense of purpose. This is the direction we are headed in answering the question which has been posed. Perhaps we can identify some choices that might bring more excitement and God-given purpose into our lives.

GOD?

Should we begin with the obvious? If you're blatantly disobeying the Bible, you're not living in God's purpose and you will experience a sense of aimlessness in your life. I think this is straightforward, so we won't spend a lot of time here.

If you wake up dreading the day or are filled with a sense of boredom and apathy about the plans you've made, you are probably not doing what you were meant to do. God gave you certain talents and a dream in your heart. He wouldn't have given you that dream and not equipped you to pursue that dream. He created you as a unique individual and He has very good plans for your life. Sure, there will be bumps along your journey, difficult things you will encounter that require patience and persistence, but generally you should look forward to your days with a sense of joy. That includes your work and your relationships.

If you are merely surviving and not living with a sense of fulfillment, you might have wandered away from your God given purpose. True fulfillment comes from doing meaningful things. Things that share the joy and excitement you find in your relationship with the Lord. Things that enrich others. Things that help the community and use the gifts God has given you. Things that tap into your passions, like a job that you can't wait to get to in the morning, or a relationship that involves real giving and receiving, and even hobbies that invigorate you. I'm not saying you won't ever have to do anything boring again, but if your entire life is gray and drab you need a change.

I think we've all been there. A pointless job. You go to work, clock in, do your thing and go home to collapse in front of the television or a video game. You find yourself working for the weekends and your eventual retirement when you will no longer have to work. Any true joy you had during that time came from hobbies or friends. How do we avoid the feeling that we are wasting our time?

Colossians 3:23-24 says, "Whatever you do, work heartily, as for the Lord and not for men, knowing that from the Lord you will receive the inheritance as your reward. You are serving the Lord Christ."

In Ecclesiastes 8:15 we read, "And I commend joy, for man has nothing better under the sun but to eat and drink and be joyful, for this will go with him in his toil through the days of his life that God has given him under the sun."

Would you say that this kind of joy and sense of purpose characterizes your life and work? If not, you might want to reevaluate where you are headed.

Perhaps you desperately want a change in your life, but you feel stuck. That's almost certainly a sign you're not walking according to God's purpose. When we are stuck and want to go in a different direction, sometimes we just don't know how to get there. We might feel like we're spinning our wheels, frustrated but unsure of how to make the frustration end, trapped. Wandering from thing to thing without any forward progress and just feeling lost.

GOD?

In his classic book, "The Lord of the Rings," J.R.R. Tolkien wrote a poem that included the line, "Not all who wander are lost." The same may apply to you. Even though you feel you are wandering without any true purpose, that doesn't necessarily mean you're lost. You can regain your sense of purpose and discover the plans God has for you.

Jeremiah 29:11 tells us God's intentions toward us, it says, "For I know the plans I have for you, declares the Lord, plans for welfare and not for evil, to give you a future and a hope."

Once again, let's begin with the obvious. If you feel as if you have no purpose, ask God to give you wisdom and direction. James 1:5 states, If any of you lacks wisdom, let him ask God, who gives generously to all without reproach, and it will be given him."

That's great news, wouldn't you say? God really wants to give you a purpose. He wants to fill you with divine wisdom. It's not like God has been holding out in order to make you miserable. He wants you to have a joyful, ambitious, purposeful life.

The primary way God speaks to us is through His Word, the Bible. This means one of the first things we need to do is start digging into Scripture in search of direction to our ultimate purpose. You aren't going to find any verses that tell you to become an athlete or a painter, but you will certainly begin to understand the heart of God.

Psalm 119:105 says, "Your Word is a lamp to my feet and a light to my path." God's Word lights up paths that are otherwise dark. The Bible teaches us how to live wisely in God's world and that is the first step toward finding your purpose.

Next, determine your personal gifts and strengths. God has given you very specific strengths and gifts. Perhaps you speak other languages. Are you a math whiz? Maybe electronics is your thing, or you have a head for business? Are you good at organizing or just getting things done? God's daily purpose for you probably involves things you're already good at. This is where you decide if further education will help in your journey, or if you just need a good YouTube video and a bit of brush up.

Now, what is something you are really passionate about? This can be anything, really. Art, economics, working with inner city youth, business, cooking, anything. If money wasn't a factor, what would you do for free? Determining your passion often helps you figure out what God has called you to do. I've heard it said that God works at the intersection of our gifts and our passions. Where do your gifts and your passions meet? That might very well be God's purpose for you.

Invite wise council. Bring others into your life who can help. Proverbs 11:14 says, "Where there is no guidance, a people falls, but in an abundance of counselors there is safety." In other words, one of the ways God can use to help you find your purpose is through others. Now, obviously your counselors should be people you trust, teachers, parents, friends, people who have your back and want the best for you.

It can be incredibly helpful to take some time of solitude. A time to think and pray. A time to really dig into the Word of God. You don't have to go to the ends of the earth or deep into the woods. Just a day away from the daily grind can be hugely rewarding. During this time allow yourself to be still, to ponder, to ask God for direction and wisdom, to listen for that still small voice. Hebrews 11:6 is a reminder that God always rewards those who seek Him. He isn't hiding from you. He wants you to seek Him out, to discover His will. He wants to guide you.

Trying to discover your life's purpose can seem almost overwhelming, but He will guide you if you ask Him to help. I have a firm belief that as a child of God our deepest purpose while we are on this earthly plain is to share the Gospel with every creature, to lift one another up and to make the world a better place while we are here. Share Jesus with everyone you meet.

Psalm 23:2-3 says, "He leads me beside still waters. He restores my soul. He leads me in paths of righteousness for His Name's sake." Trust God. You may feel confused, but God doesn't.

Why am I Here?

We've all asked this question in moments of fear, in times of darkness, when we feel as though no matter what we do its never right, when we have felt unloved and forsaken. I know there have been times in my own life when I've wondered, "What earthly good am I?" "Why was I born?" And of course, the famous, "Would anyone miss me if I were gone?" I praise God that those thoughts no longer plague me, but I wonder if anyone out there still feels this way?

I want you to know that God loves you. If you were the only human being on earth, He would still have thought you valuable enough to come to earth and die for you on that cross at Calvary. And because He died and rose again you can be made whole, your sin erased, your rough edges polished and shined.

Because He rose again and sits at the right hand of the Father in Heaven, you can have a brand-new life. You can know without a doubt that you are righteous and worthy, through Him, if you simply BELIEVE. Put your faith in the only one in the universe perfect and holy enough to be held up as the ultimate sacrifice. The only one willing to offer up His life for you. The one who took the stripes on His own back that were meant for yours, to pay for your physical healing; the one who wore the crown of thorns meant for your brow, in order to give you mental peace; the only one willing to suffer the nails pounded into His hands and feet to pay for your sins and mine. My Lord, my Savior, my Jesus.

7 Prophesies Which Must be Fulfilled Before the Coming of Christ

Here are the prophesies I promised you in the beginning of this book. I believe you will find them fascinating. As you read through you will likely notice that some have already been brought to fruition and others could be accomplished as any moment. The soon coming of Jesus Christ could easily happen in our lifetime. Praise the Lord.

#1 The human race will have the ability to exterminate itself (Matthew 24:22).

#2 A Jewish homeland had to be reestablished

in the Middle East (Luke 21:7, 20-22, Zechariah 12:2-3, 9, 14' Zechariah 14:1-4, 16, Daniel 12:1-13 and Daniel 11:31, Matthew 24:15.

#3 The end-time king of the North and king of the South (Daniel 11 an amazing prophesy about the kings of the areas North and South of the Holy Land, which is fleshed out in Daniel 8:3,5 and 8).

#4 An end-time union of European nations (In Daniel 2 and 7 we see prophecies about four great gentile empires that would arise in the period between the time of Daniel and the coming establishment of the Kingdom of God [Daniel 2:44]. Daniel, himself, was living in the first of these great empires [Daniel 7:4] as a Jewish exile in ancient Babylon. Following the fall of Babylon in 539 B.C., Persia would become the greatest power, to be followed by Greece [Daniel 7:5-6]. After Greece came the Roman empire, "dreadful and terrible, exceedingly strong." This empire was to have "ten horns" (leaders or governments) and would continue in some form until the establishment of God's Kingdom at Christ's return [Daniel 7:7-9]. The ten horns symbolize ten attempts to restore the Roman Empire to the power it had in ancient times. Various attempts at a restoration have taken place since the fall of the Western Roman Empire in A.D. 476. A final attempt will be made shortly before Christ's return [European Union?])

We find more detail in Revelation 17. We read of a final attempt to revive the Roman Empire by "ten kings who have received no kingdom as yet, but they receive authority for one hour as kings with the beast. These are of one mind, and they will give their power and authority to the beast" (Revelation 17:12-13). They will also "make war with the Lamb [Jesus Christ], and the Lamb will overcome them, for He is Lord of lords and King of kings" (Revelation 17:14). Clearly this prophecy is still to be realized.

Previous attempts to forge a united European empire, from Justinian in the sixth century through Charlemagne, Napoleon, Mussolini and Hitler, all involved force. The final resurrection of the Roman Empire will not be attempted in the same way. Revelation 17 suggests this is a voluntary union. When these ten leaders receive power, they will then give their authority to a single leader. Scripture refers to both this individual and the new superpower he leads as "the beast" - acknowledging it as a continuation of the four gentile empires prophesied in Daniel. Only now, in this day and age, is it possible for this prophesy to be fulfilled.

#5 End-time rise and fall of Israel and Judah. Understanding critical parts of Biblical history helps us more fully comprehend a passage of Scripture in the book of Hosea, which is a prophecy about Ephraim (the multitude of nations – Great Britain and some of those nations that came out of her). It warns of destruction to follow the end-time ascendancy of the Israelite nations. In Hosea 5 we read a prophecy that mentions Israel, Ephraim and Judah (Judah refers to the Jewish people, particularly those who now constitute the modern nation of Israel.): "The pride of Israel testifies to his face;

therefore, Israel and Ephraim stumble in their iniquity; Judah also stumbles with them" (Hosea 5:5). The prophesy continues: "With their flocks and herds they shall go to seek the Lord, but they will not find Him; He has withdrawn Himself from them. They have dealt treacherously with the Lord, for they have begotten pagan children. Now a New Moon shall devour them and their heritage" (Hosea 5:6-7).

Since new moons occur a month apart, a new moon "devouring" them would seem to mean that Israel, Ephraim and Judah will all fall within one month.

Remember that Israel gave his name to Ephraim and Manasseh, the ancestors in turn of the British and American peoples. As Ephraim is mentioned separately in this prophecy, the reference to "Israel" must apply to the United States, which is now the more dominant of the two nations. This prophecy was not fulfilled in the past, since ancient Judah fell to Babylon more than a century after Israel fell to Assyria. Yet in the end it appears they will fall together – within one month of each other. This prophecy has yet to be fulfilled.

#6 The Gospel will be preached in all the world. In His major end-time prophecy, Jesus answers the question posed by the disciples: "When will these things be? And what will be the sign of your coming, and the end of the age?" (Matthew 24:3). After listing a number of signs of the nearness of His coming, He reveals that "this Gospel of the kingdom will be preached in all the world as a witness to all the nations, and then the end will come" (Matthew 24:14).

It has only become possible within the past fifty years or so to reach all countries with various forms of communication. Even so, there are communist regimes that do not allow their citizens the right to freedom of religion. China, for instance, with over a quarter of the world's population does not. However, the internet is changing things. It is much harder for governments to control what their people can and cannot see and the Gospel message is still going out to the world. This is a prophecy whose time has come.

#7 Instant worldwide communications and God's final witnesses. Only with the technical advances of the last few years has it become possible for the events in Revelation 11 to occur

– for people around the world to see the fate of God's two final witnesses. These two witnesses, reminiscent of other biblical prophets like Elijah and Elisha, will carry God's final warning to the world in the last three and a half years leading up to Christ's return. "And I will give power to my two witnesses, and they will prophesy one thousand two hundred and sixty days…When they finish their testimony, the beast that ascends out of the bottomless pit will make war against them, overcome them and kill them. And their dead bodies will lie in the street of the great city which spiritually is called Sodom and Egypt, where also our Lord was crucified. Then those from the peoples, tribes, tongues and nations will see their dead bodies three-and-a-half days, and not allow their dead bodies to be put into graves.

And those who dwell on the earth will rejoice over them, make merry, and send gifts to one another, because these two prophets tormented those who dwell on the earth" (Revelation 11:3, Revelation 11:7-10).

The accomplishment of this prophecy would not have been possible before satellite television, cell phones and the internet. Again, only in the last few years has it become possible for this prophecy to be fulfilled. It still lies in the future, of course, but it is clearly possible for this to take place.

All has now become possible. This, in turn, makes it much more likely that our generation will live to see Jesus Christ return and establish the Kingdom of God on earth. After all, Jesus Himself said that once these things begin, the generation alive at that time "will by no means pass away till all these things take place" (Matthew 24:34).

As Jesus tells His followers in Luke 21:28, "Now when these things begin to happen, look up and lift up your heads, because your redemption draws near."

As I ponder the words of Luke in chapter 21 and verse 28 my eyes tear up in hopeful expectation. Yes, I know that no man will know the exact moment of Jesus' return, but it certainly seems nearby, doesn't it? With all the prophetic signs of His imminent return playing out around us I can't help but be excited. If you know Christ as your personal Savior, you should be excited too. We are living in tumultuous times, yes, but they are also wonderful times as we watch end time scenarios take shape. Now, we must quickly be about our Father's business.

In Matthew 28:19-20 we read, "And Jesus came and said to them, "All authority in heaven and on earth has been given to me. Go therefore and make disciples of all nations, baptizing them in the Name of the Father and of the Son and of the Holy Spirit, teaching them to observe all that I have commanded you. And behold, I am with you always, to the end of the age."

Mark 16:15-18 says, "And He said to them, go into all the world and proclaim the Gospel to the whole creation. Whoever believes and is baptized will be saved, but whoever does not believe will be condemned. And these signs will accompany those who believe in My Name they will cast our demons; they will speak in new tongues; they will pick up serpents with their hands; and if they drink any deadly poison, it will not hurt them; they will lay hands on the sick, and they will recover."

I think that makes our assignment here on earth pretty clear, don't you? We are commanded to share Jesus with the world and that can start in your own backyard. Do you have a family member, friend, co-worker, neighbor, anyone, who does not know Jesus as Savior and Lord? Now is the time.

My own greatest desire is to share Jesus with every person I meet. I bought a t-shirt recently that is screen printed with the words, "Warning, I may start talking about Jesus at any time." The first time I wore it several people commented, "Boy, that's the truth." I guess I talk about Jesus a lot and that might seem a bit annoying to some people. I don't care. How can I have within my knowledge the best thing, the best person, the most exciting message in the universe and not share? That would be beyond selfish in my humble opinion.

If you had the cure for cancer and didn't make your way to the cancer center to share the miracle with everyone there, that would be selfish. However, as a Christian, I (we) have knowledge of the cure for everything that ails the world, every sin, every illness, every disease, every emotional distress, every worry. His Name is Jesus and I simply cannot keep Him to myself.

God bless you. He loves you, now children of the King, go ye and proclaim His grace to the world.

www.ingramcontent.com/pod-product-compliance
Lightning Source LLC
Chambersburg PA
CBHW071952110526
44592CB00012B/1060